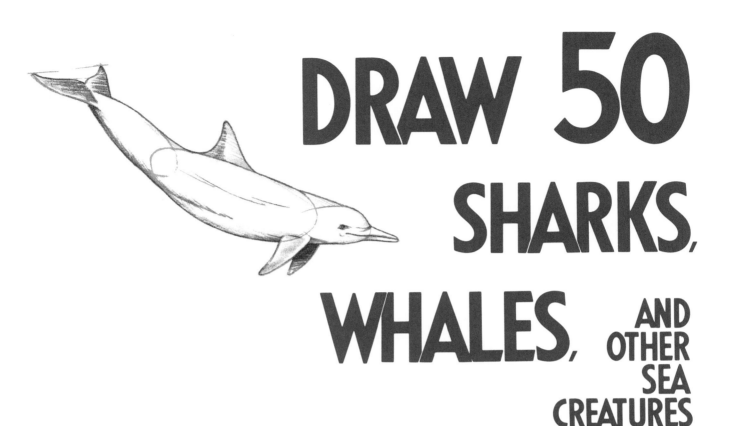

DRAW 50

SHARKS,

WHALES, AND OTHER SEA CREATURES

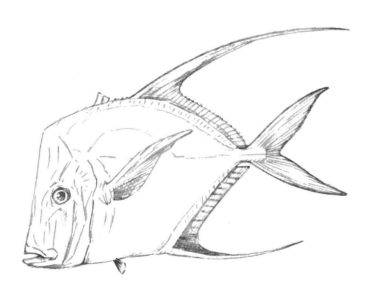

BOOKS IN THIS SERIES

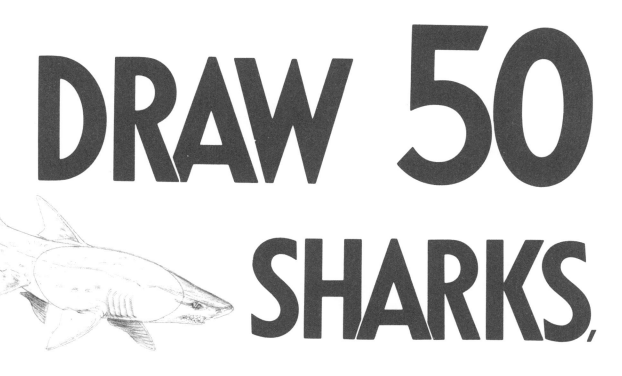

DRAW 50
SHARKS,
WHALES, AND OTHER SEA CREATURES

LEE J. AMES
with Warren Budd

BROADWAY BOOKS
NEW YORK

BROADWAY

Published by Broadway Books
a division of Random House, Inc.
1540 Broadway, New York, New York 10036

BROADWAY BOOKS and it's logo, a letter B bisected on the diagonal, are
trademarks of Broadway Books, a division of Random House, Inc.

Library of Congress Cataloging-in-Publication Data
Ames, Lee J.
   Draw 50 sharks, whales, and other sea creatures / Lee J. Ames with
Warren Budd.—1st ed.
        p.   cm.
   Summary: Provides step-by-step instructions for drawing a variety
of sharks, whales, and other sea creatures, including the hammerhead
shark, humpback whale, and giant sea turtle.
   1. Sharks in art—Juvenile literature. 2. Whales in art—Juvenile
literature. 3. Marine fauna in art—Juvenile literature.
4. Drawing—Technique—Juvenile literature. [1. Sharks in art.
2. Whales in art. 3. Marine animals in art. 4. Drawing—
Technique.] I. Budd, Warren. II. Title. III. Title: Draw
fifty sharks, whales, and other sea creatures.
NC781.A44   1989
743'.6—dc19   88-35163
CIP
AC
ISBN: 0-385-24627-7
        0-385-24628-5 (lib. bdg.)
        0-385-26768-1 (pbk.)

26 25 24 23 22 21 20

To Warren, with great appreciation
for the wonderful job that you've done,
and there's nothing fishy about that remark.
L.J.A.

To Lee,
with thanks for the opportunity.
W.B.

TO THE READER

Perhaps by now you have come across one of my "Draw 50" books, or perhaps this is the first one you've ever picked up. Either way, I hope to show you in this book how to draw a wide variety of fascinating sea creatures. I have a great love and respect for the other creatures of this earth and for that reason, I've chosen to go underwater and give you a sampling of the wonderful life-forms that live there.

At first glance, the drawings in this book may appear difficult. But if you take your time and carefully follow the step-by-step instructions for each illustration, you will be able to produce a satisfying finished drawing.

To begin, you will need only clean paper, a pencil with moderately soft lead (HB or No. 2), and a kneaded eraser (available at art supply stores). Select the illustration you want to draw, and then *very lightly and carefully*, sketch out step number one. Then, also very *lightly and carefully*, add step number two to step number one. These steps, which may look the easiest, are the most important. A mistake here can ruin your entire drawing at the end. And remember to watch not only the lines themselves, but the *spaces between the lines* to make sure that they are the same as for the drawing in the book. As you sketch out these first steps, it might be a good idea to hold your work up to a mirror. Sometimes the mirror shows that you've twisted the drawing off to one side without being aware of it.

In each drawing, the new step is shown darker than the previous one so that it can be clearly seen. But you should keep your own work very light. Here's where the kneaded eraser will come in handy; use it to lighten your work after each step.

When you have finished your picture, you may want to go over it with some India ink. Apply this with a fine brush or pen. When the ink has thoroughly dried, erase the entire drawing with the kneaded eraser. The erasing will not affect the India ink.

The most important thing to remember is that even if your first attempts are not as good as you would like them to be, you should not get discouraged. Like any other talent, whether it be performing gymnastic feats or playing the piano, drawing takes practice to do your best.

Though there are many ways to learn how to draw, the step-by-step method used in this book should start you off in the right direction.

LEE J. AMES

TO THE PARENT OR TEACHER

"Leslie can draw the best Great White Shark I ever saw!" Such peer acclaim and encouragement generate incentive. Contemporary methods of art instruction (freedom of expression, experimentation, self-evaluation of competence and growth) provide a vigorous, fresh-air approach for which we must all be grateful.

New ideas need not, however, totally exclude the old. One such is the "follow me, step-by-step" approach. In my young learning days this method was so common, and frequently so exclusive, that the student became nothing more than a pantographic extension of the teacher. In those days it was excessively overworked.

This does not mean that the young hand is never to be guided. Rather, specific guiding is fundamental. Step-by-step guiding that produces satisfactory results is valuable even when the means of accomplishment are not fully understood by the student.

The novice with a musical instrument is frequently taught to play simple melodies as quickly as possible, well before he or she learns the most elemental scratchings at the surface of music theory. The resultant self-satisfaction, pride in accomplishment, can provide significant motivation. And all from mimicking an instructor's "Do-as-I-do . . ."

Mimicry is prerequisite for developing creativity. We learn the use of our tools by mimicry. Then we can use those tools for creativity. To this end I would offer the budding artist the opportunity to memorize or mimic (rote-like, if you wish) the making of "pictures"—"pictures" he or she has been anxious to be able to draw.

The use of this book should be available to anyone who *wants* to try another way of flapping his or her wings. Perhaps he or she will then get off the ground when a friend says, "Leslie can draw the best Great White Shark I ever saw!"

LEE J. AMES

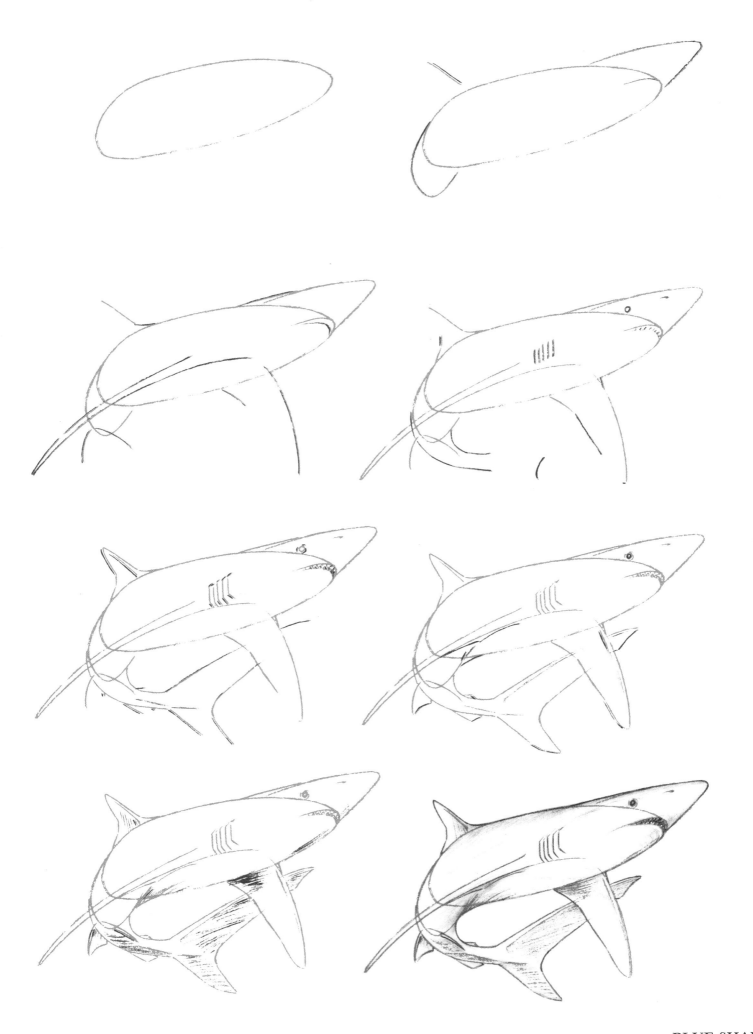

BLUE SHARK
Up to ten feet long

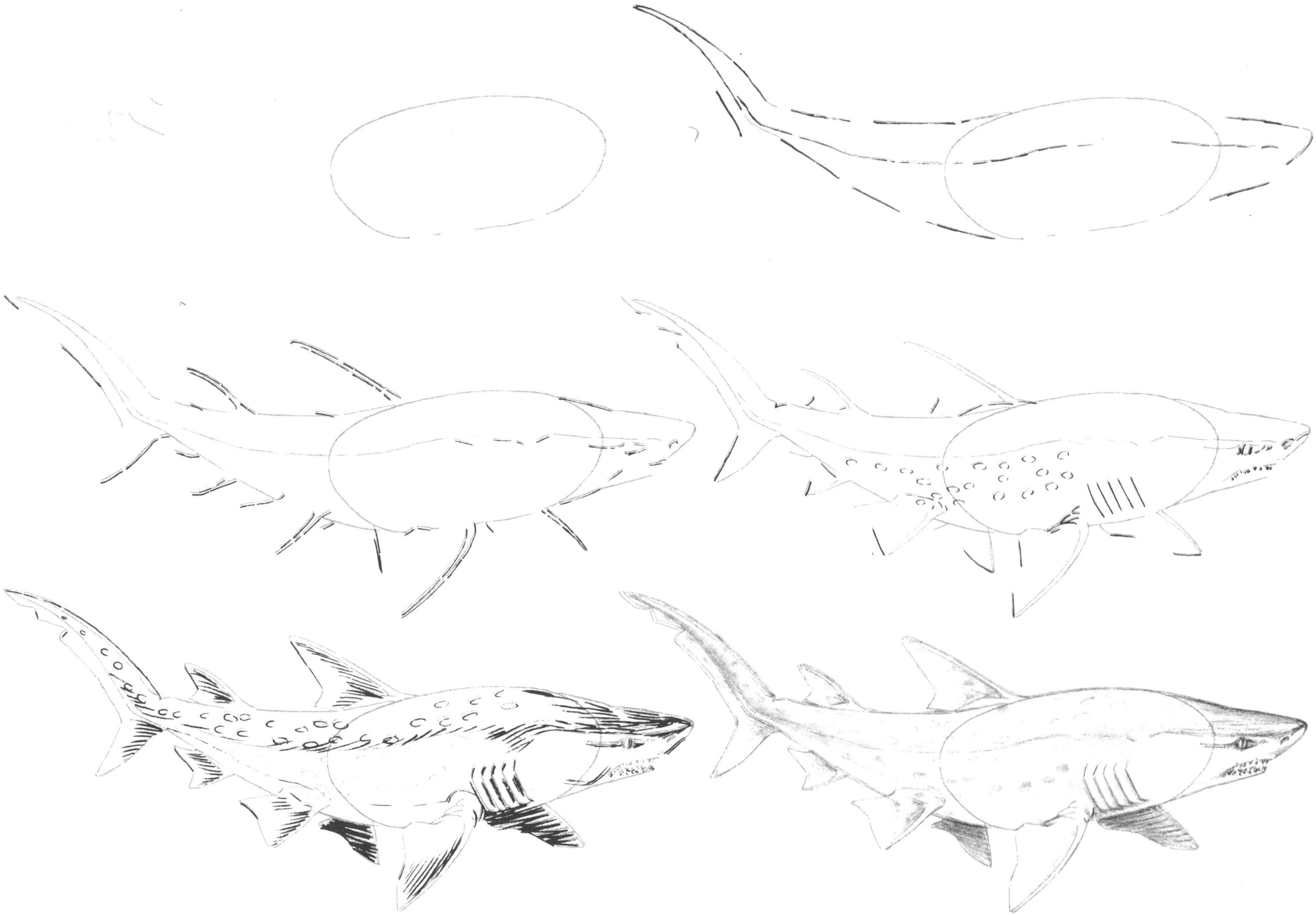

SAND TIGER SHARK
Six to seven feet long

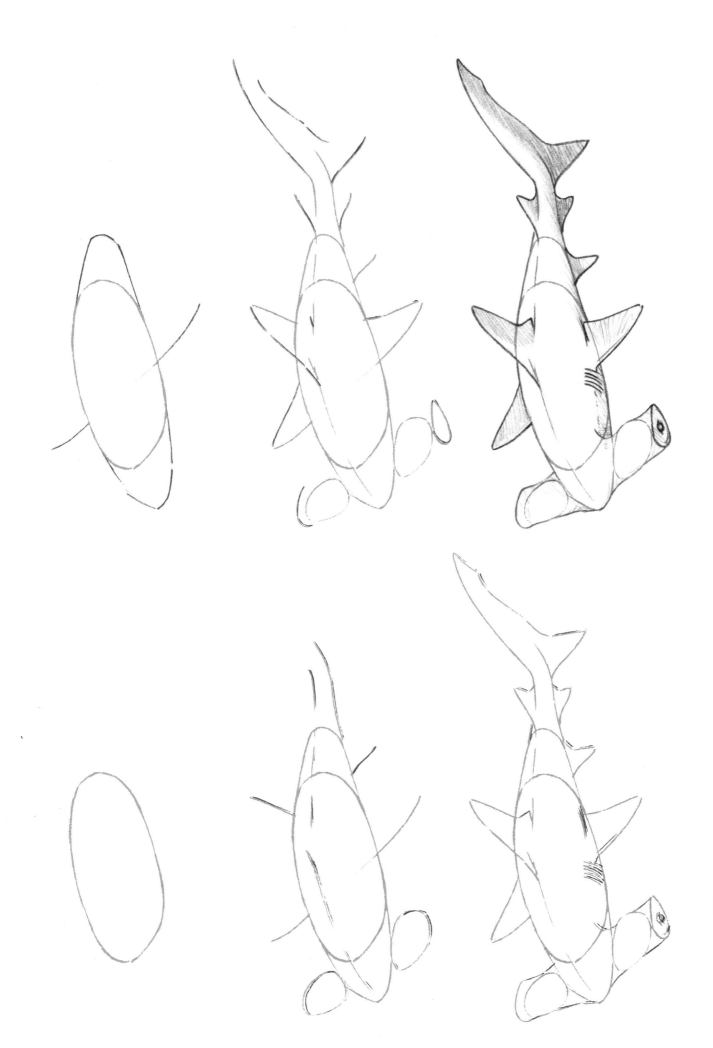

HAMMERHEAD SHARK
Up to twenty feet long

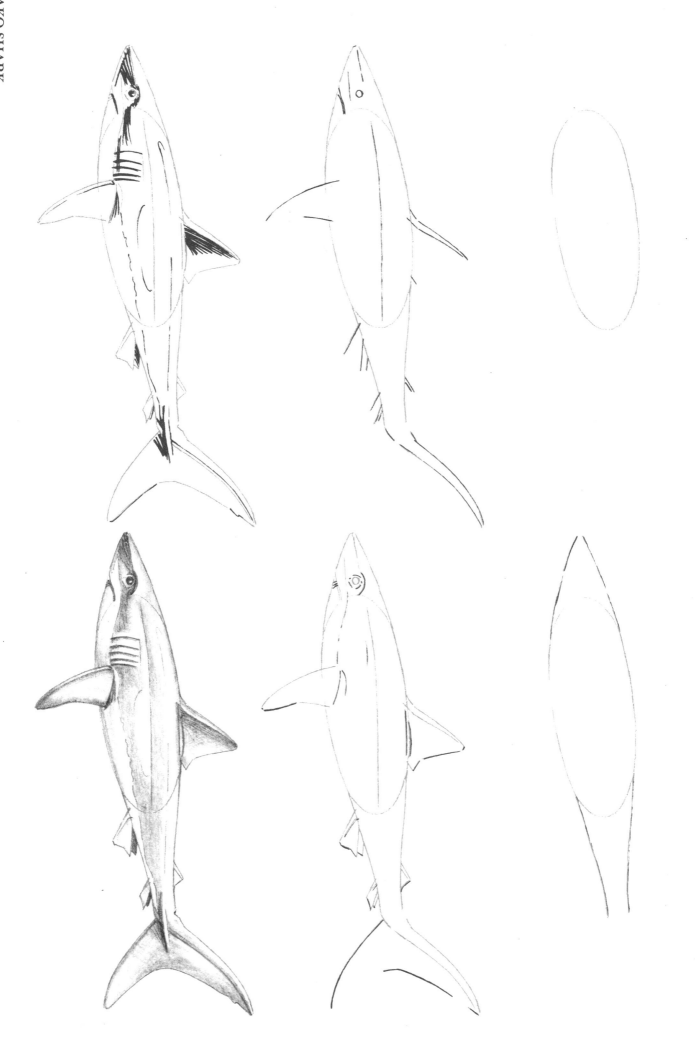

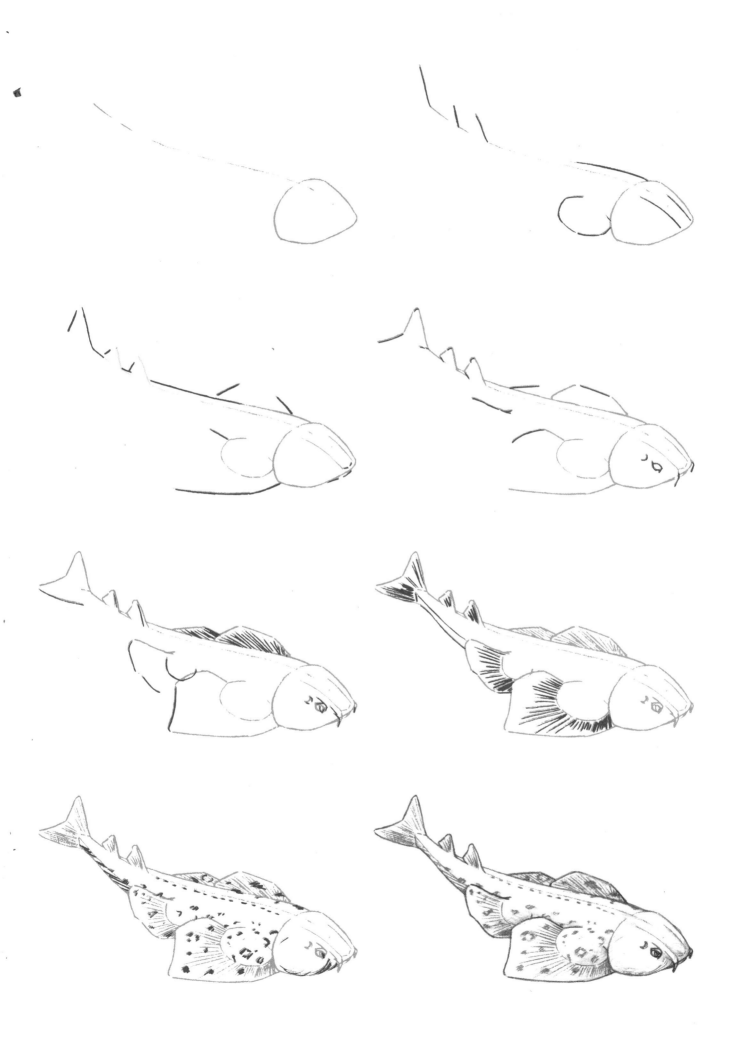

PACIFIC ANGEL SHARK
Up to five feet long

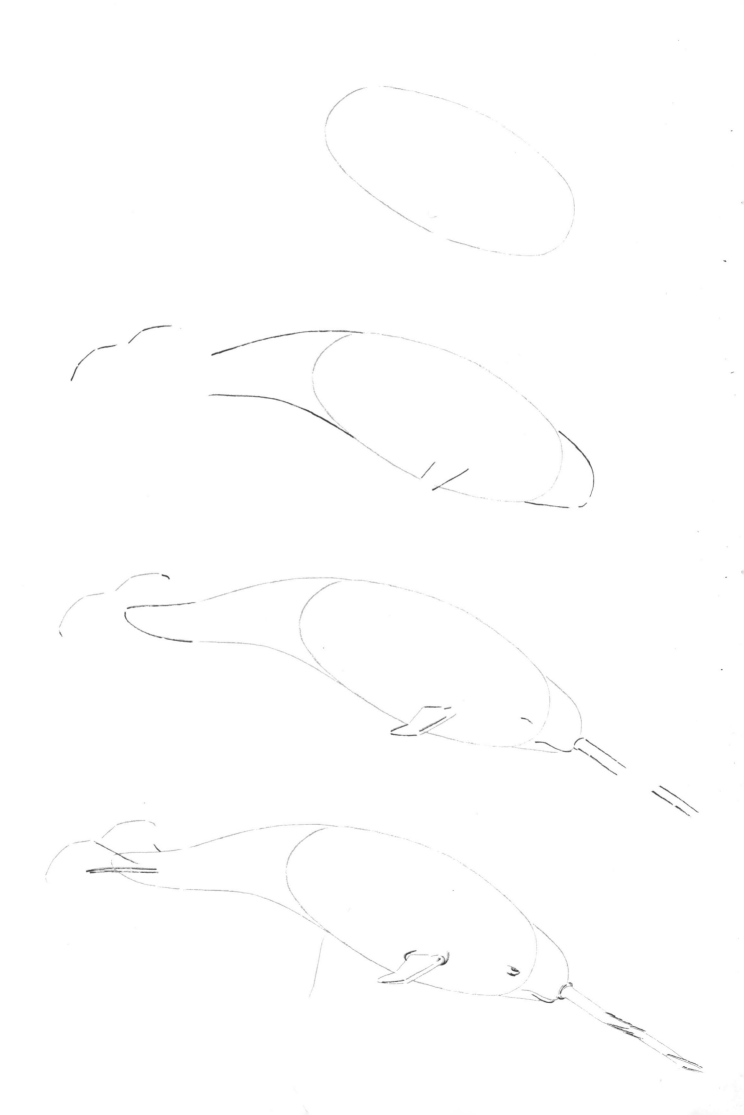

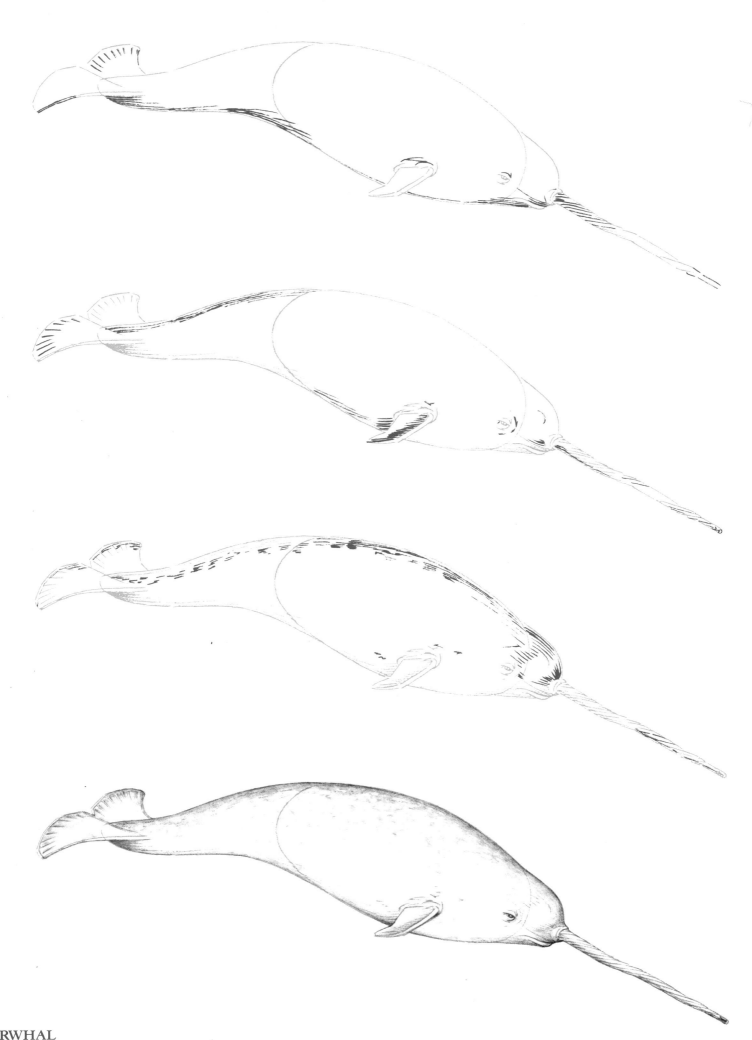

ARWHAL

Up to fifteen feet long, with the horn sometimes growing to nine feet

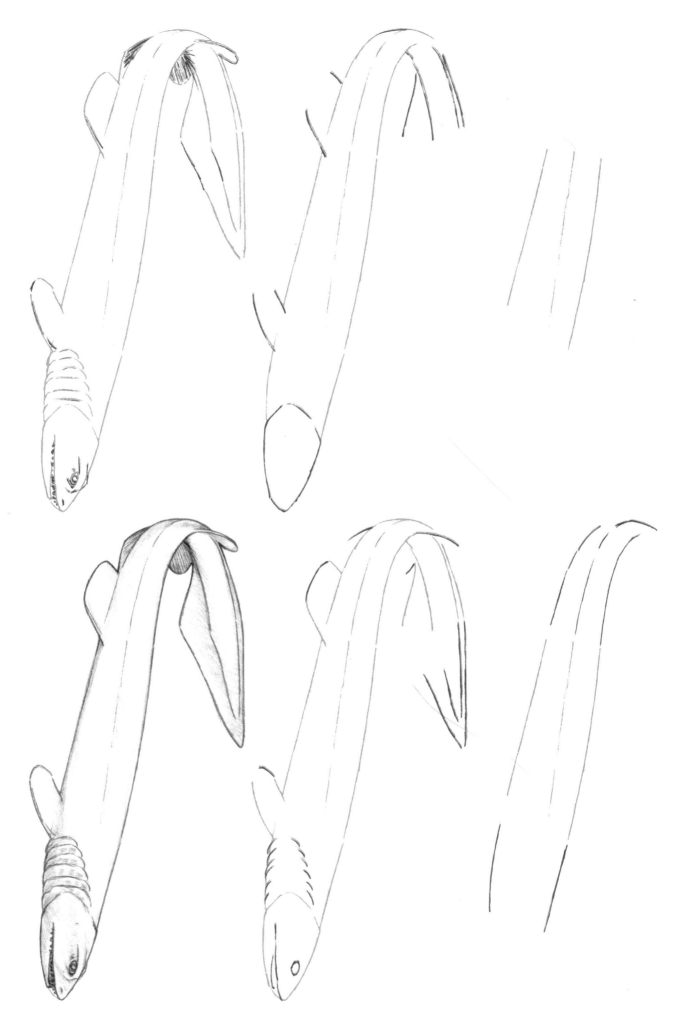

FRILLED SHARK
Five to six feet long

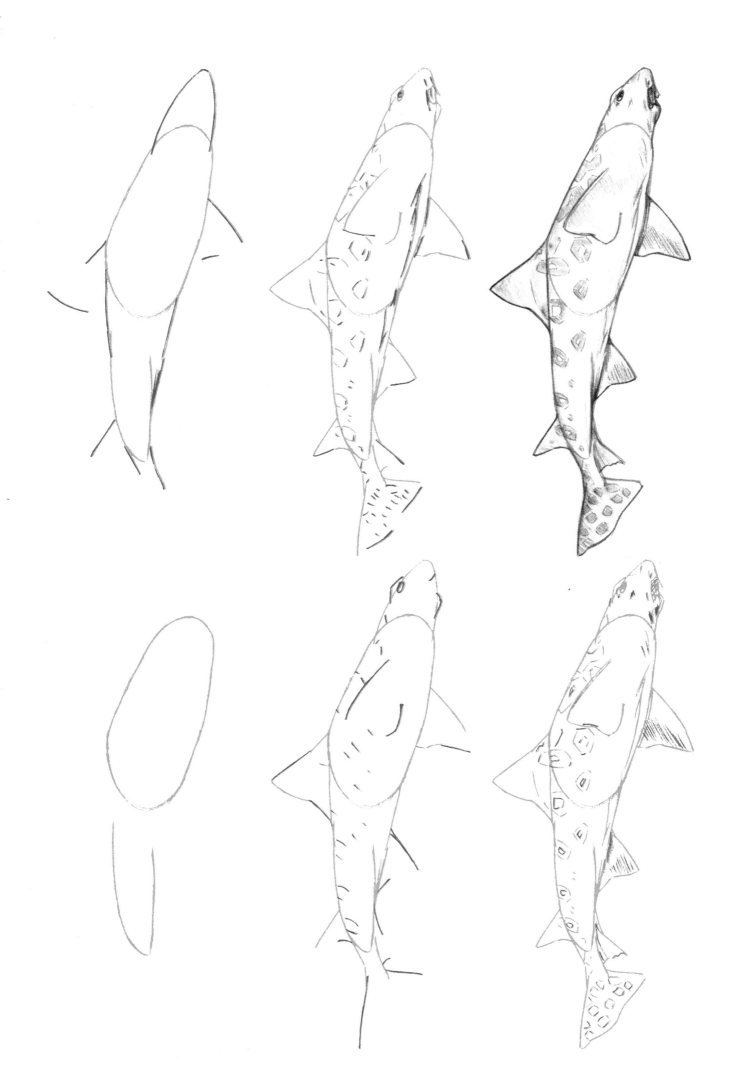

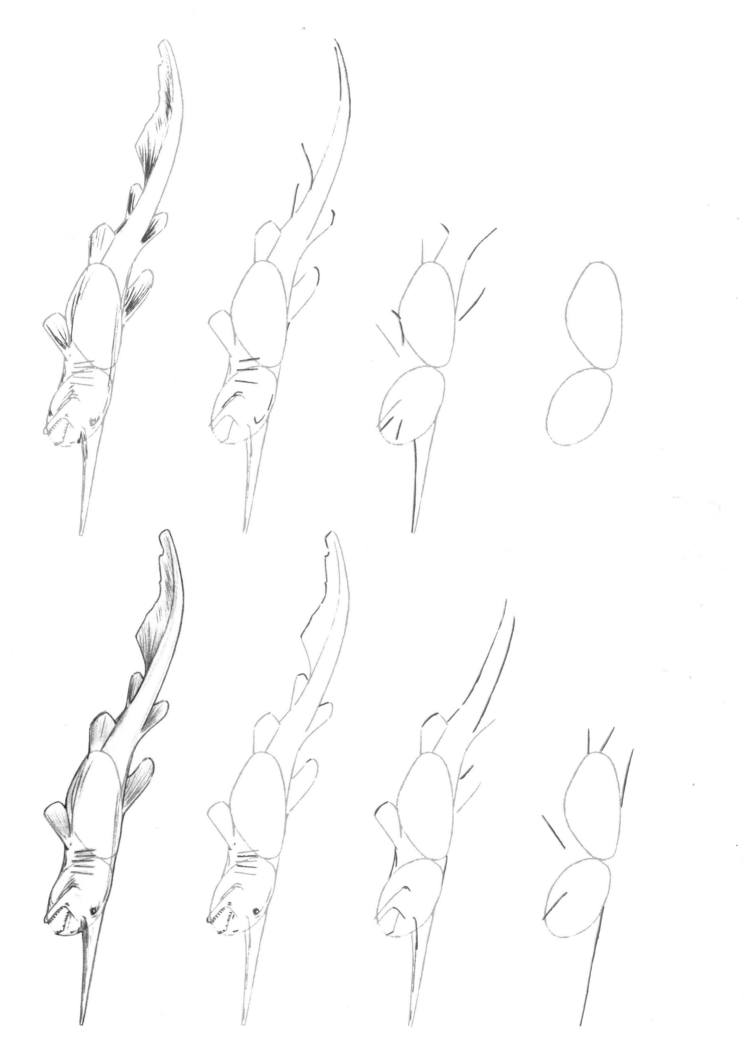

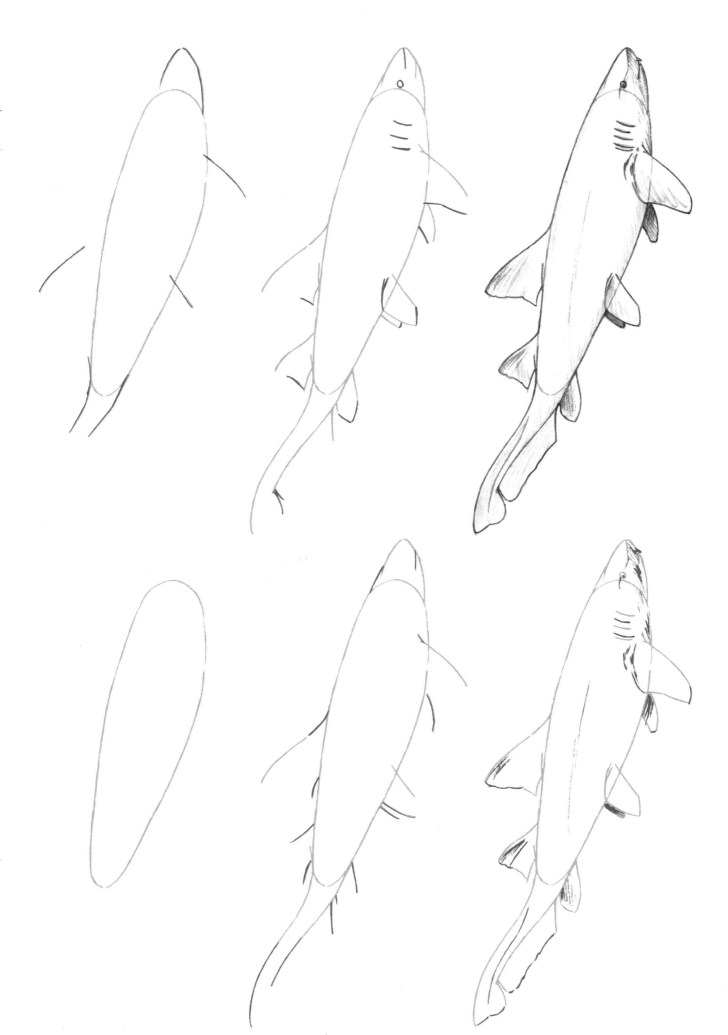

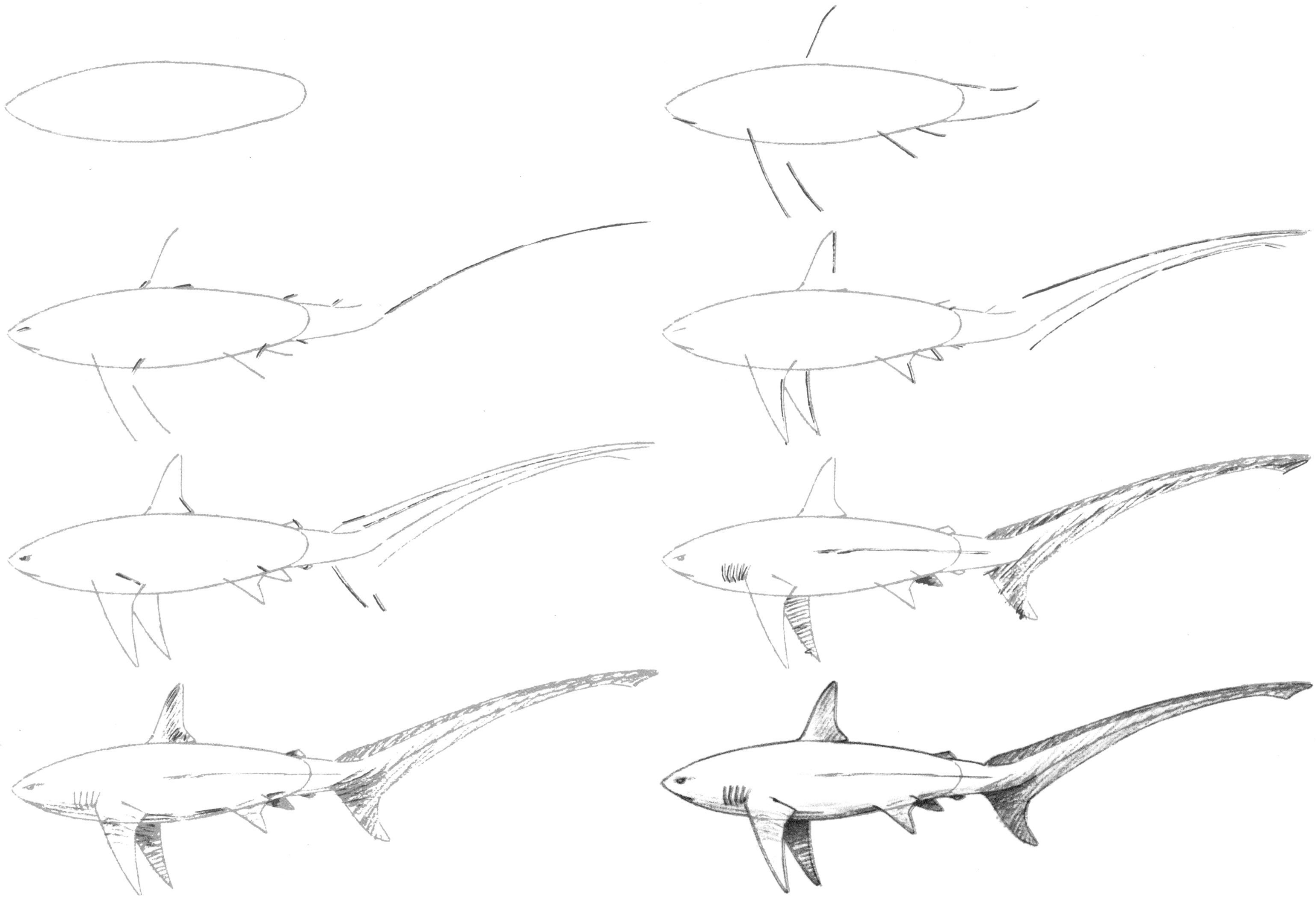

THRESHER SHARK

Up to twenty-five feet long

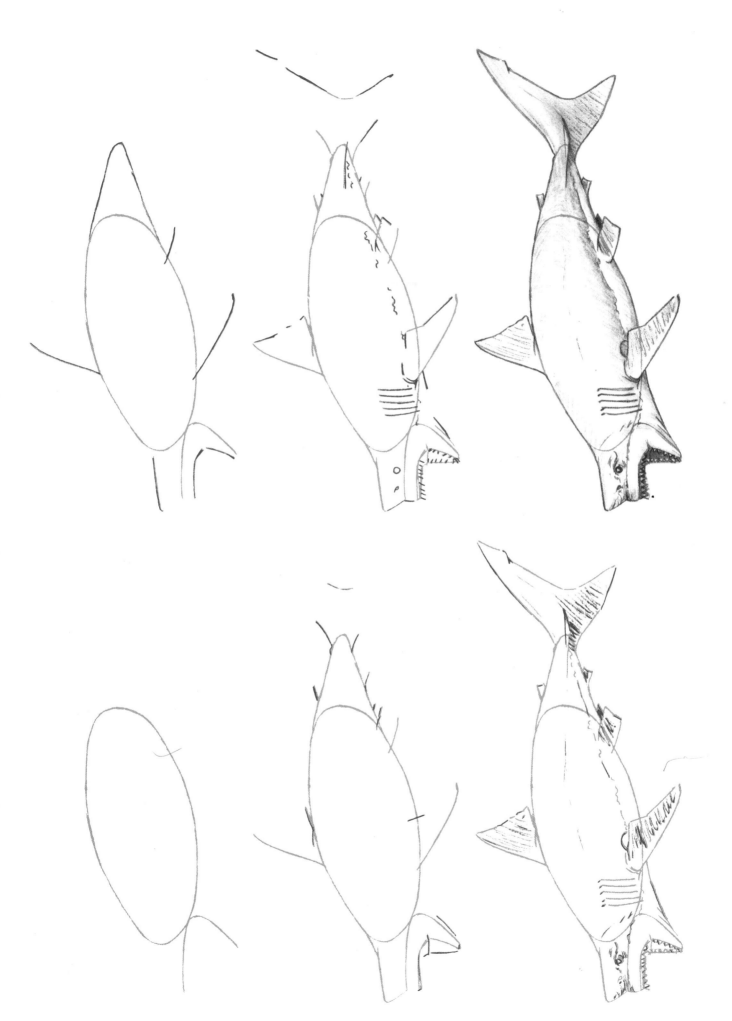

GREAT WHITE SHARK
Up to twenty-five feet long

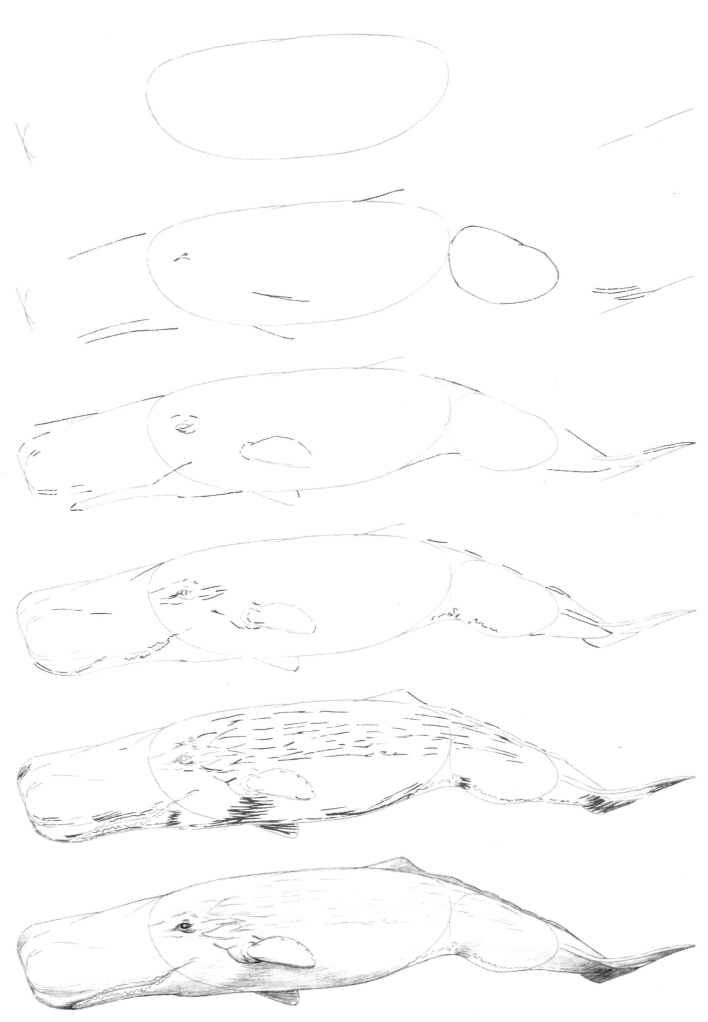

SPERM WHALE

Up to sixty-one feet long

Courtesy of *National Geographic*
From a photo by Flip Nicklin

KILLER WHALE
Up to thirty feet long

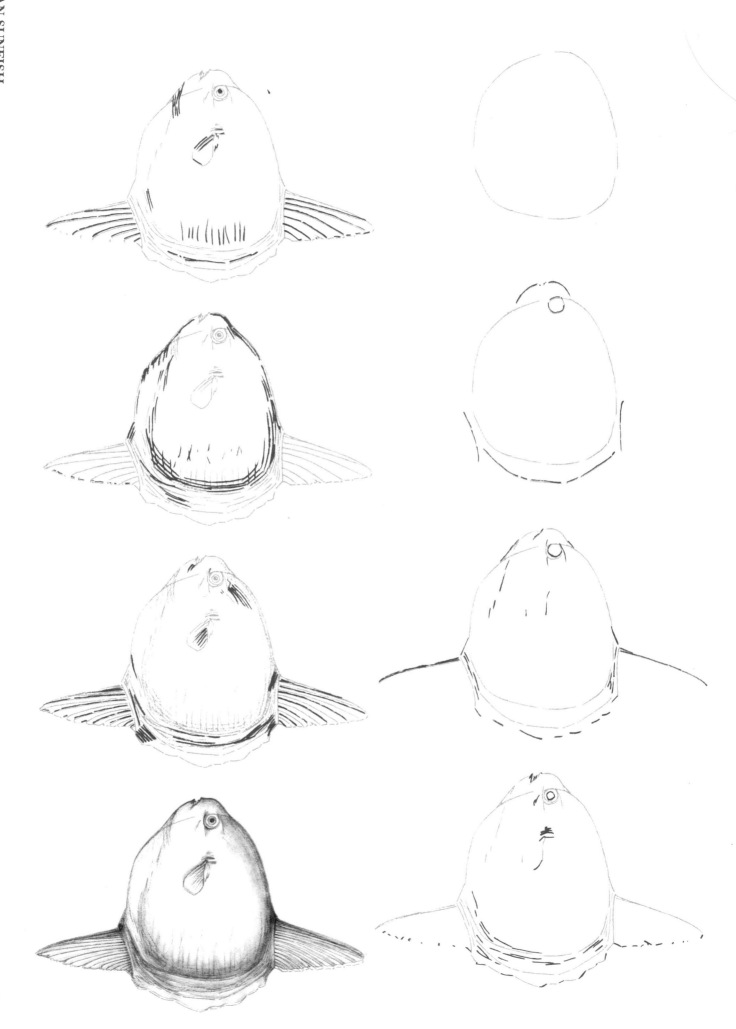

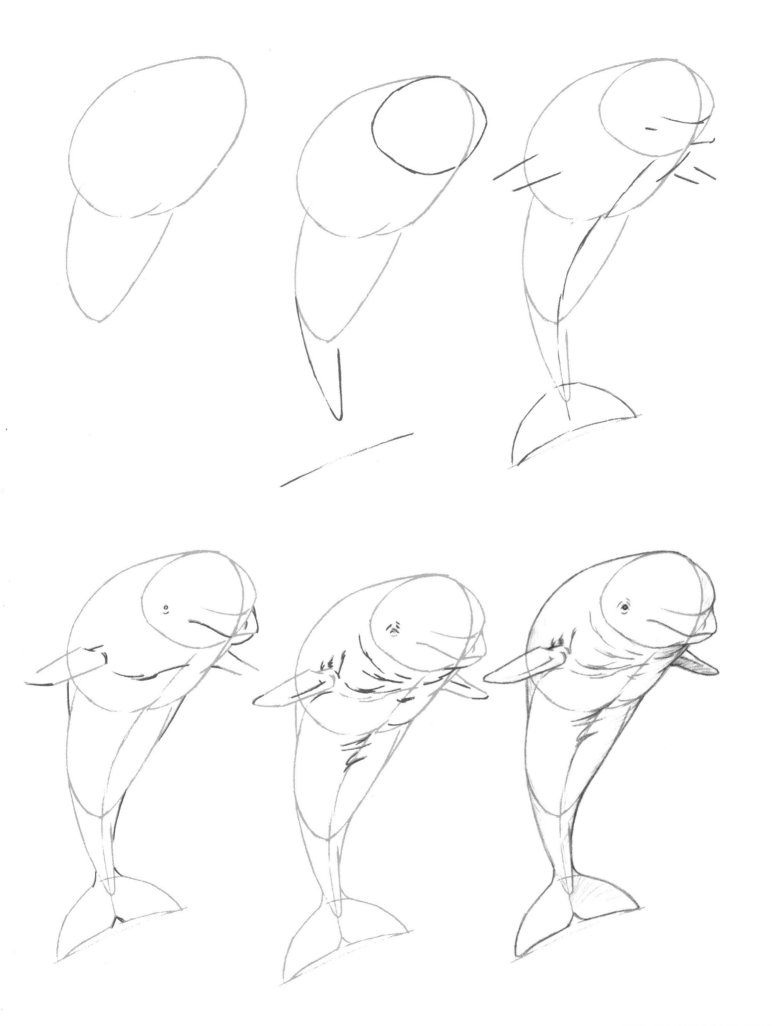

WHITE (BELUGA) WHALE
Up to twenty feet long

An ancient giant fish, up to twenty-seven feet long

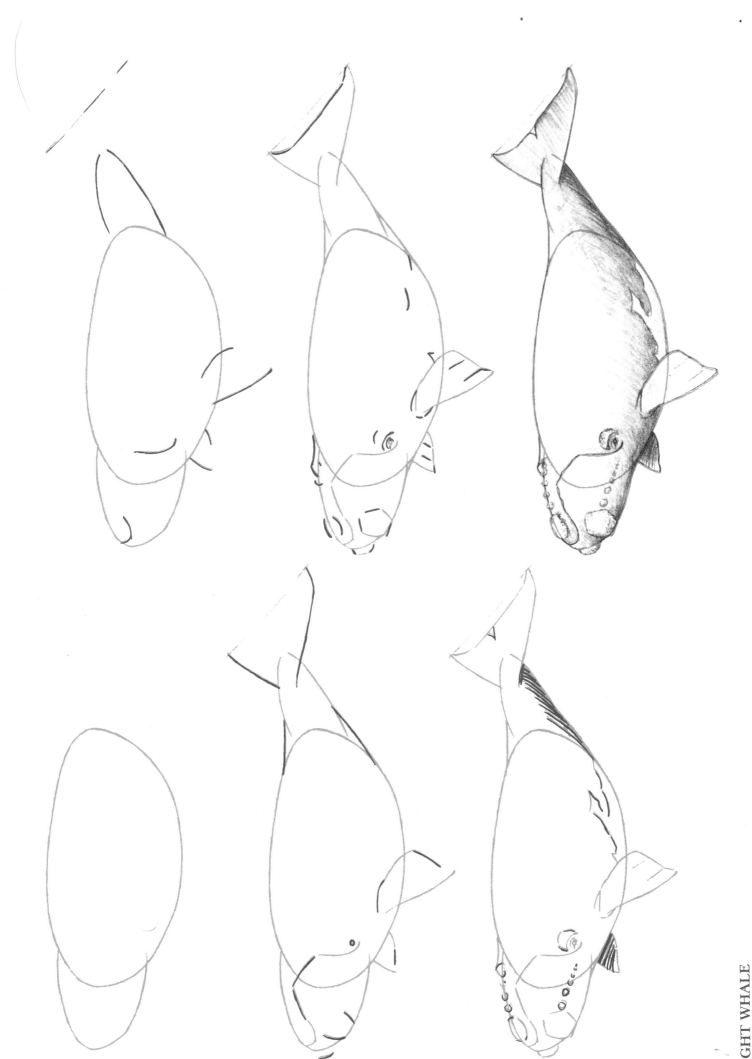

RIGHT WHALE
Up to sixty feet long

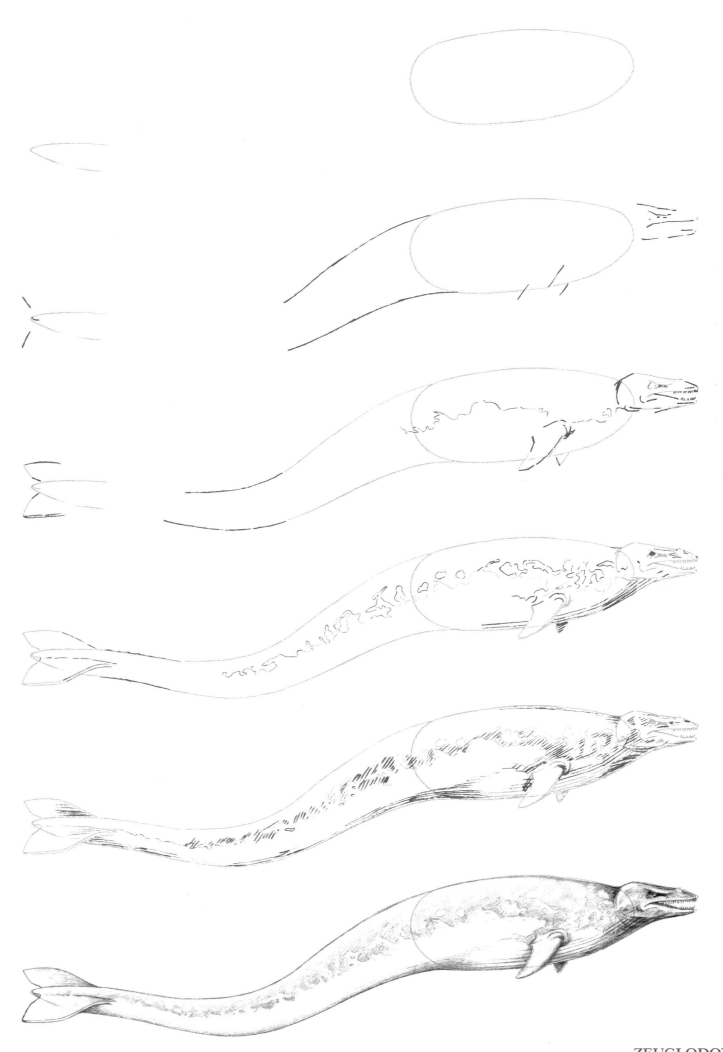

ZEUGLODO

A primitive whale, up to sixty-five feet lon

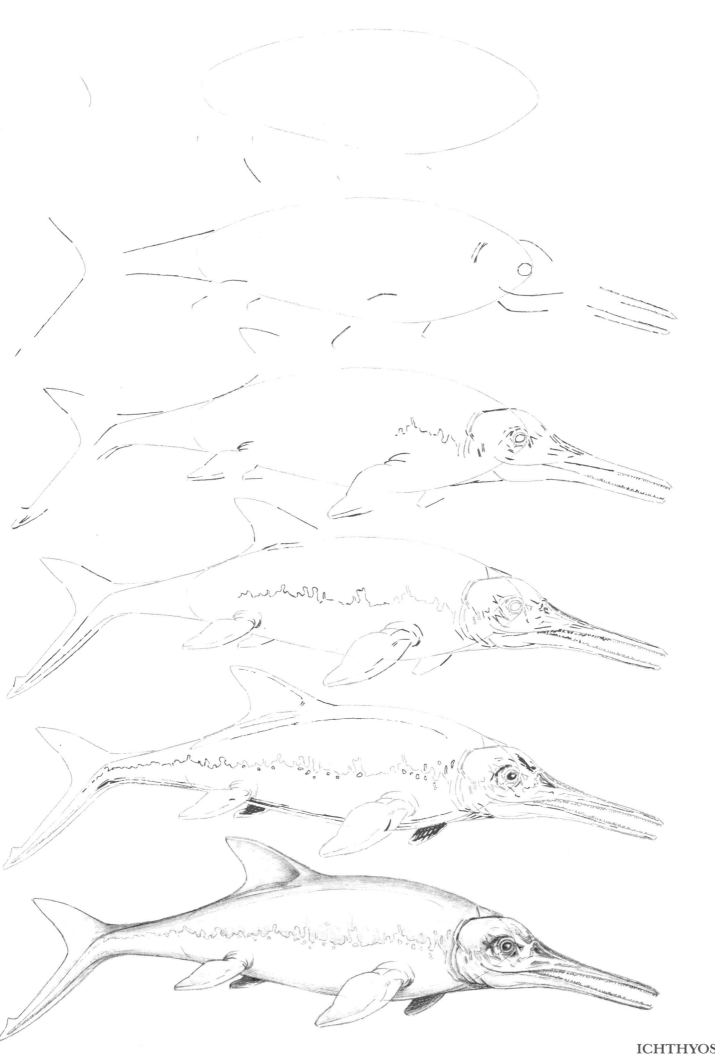

ICHTHYOSAUR
A seagoing reptile, up to forty feet long

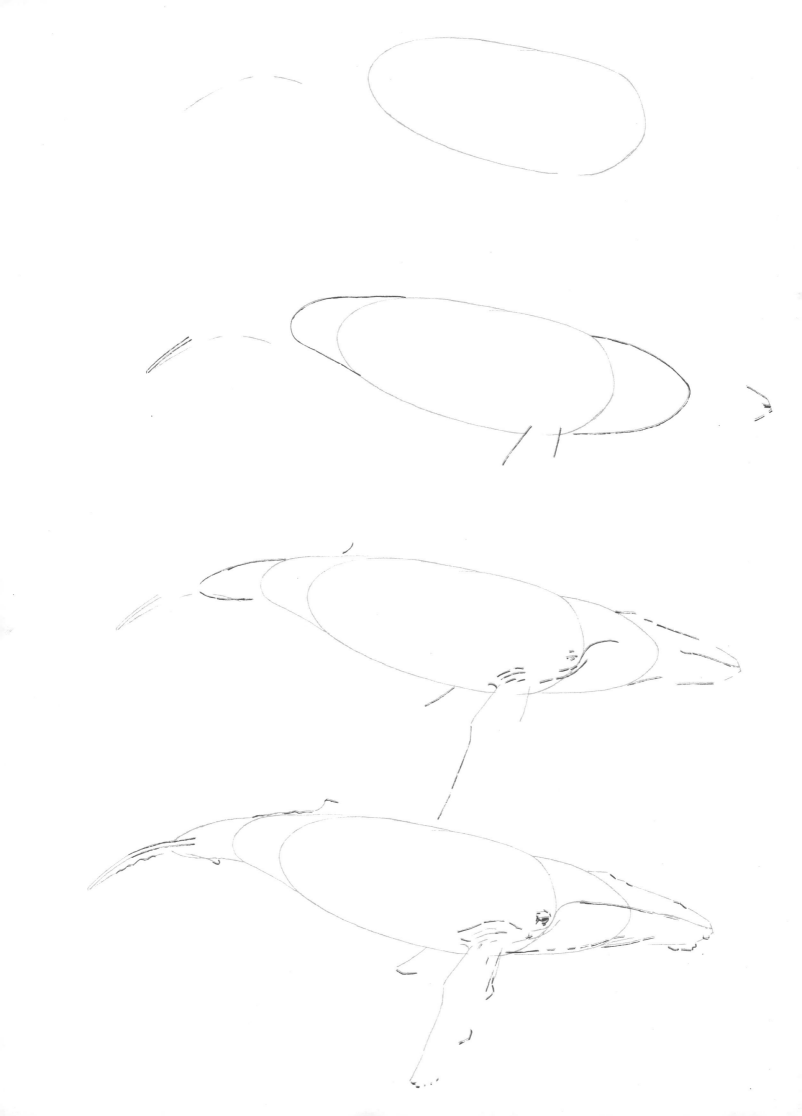

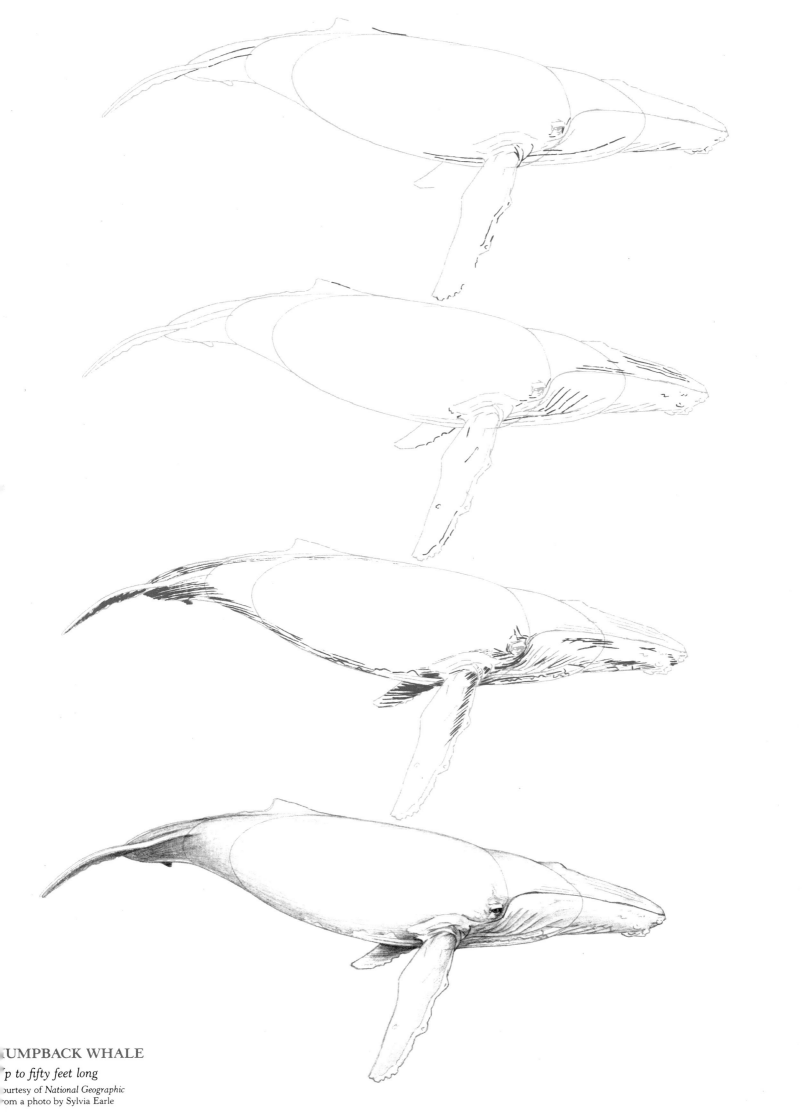

HUMPBACK WHALE

up to fifty feet long

Courtesy of *National Geographic*
from a photo by Sylvia Earle

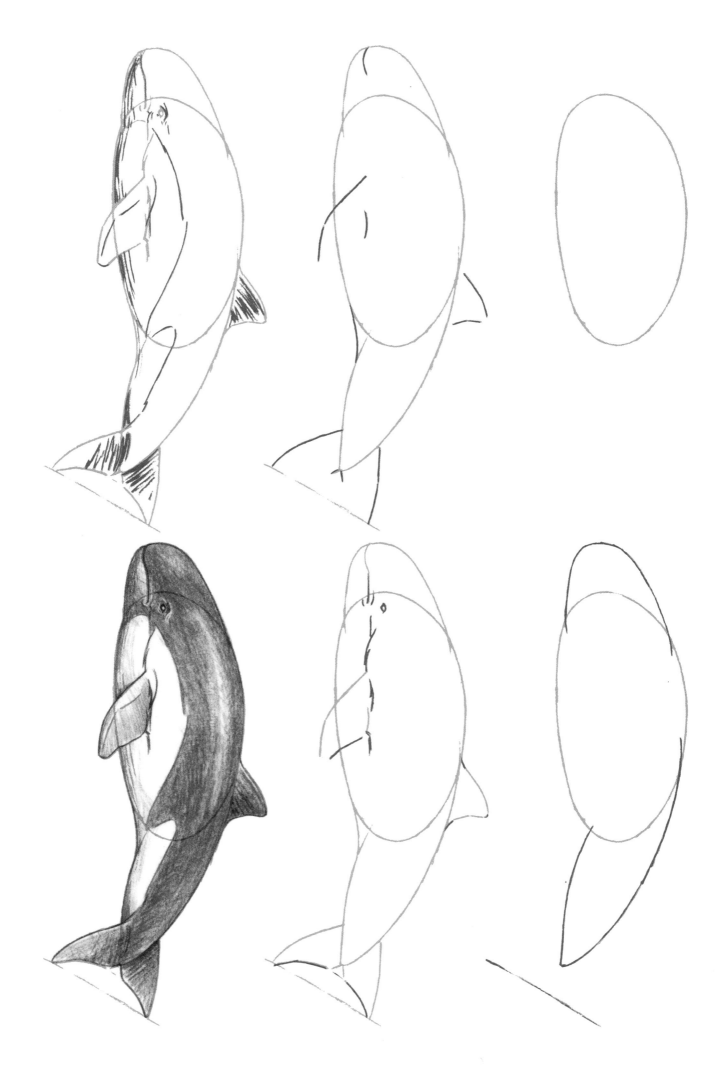

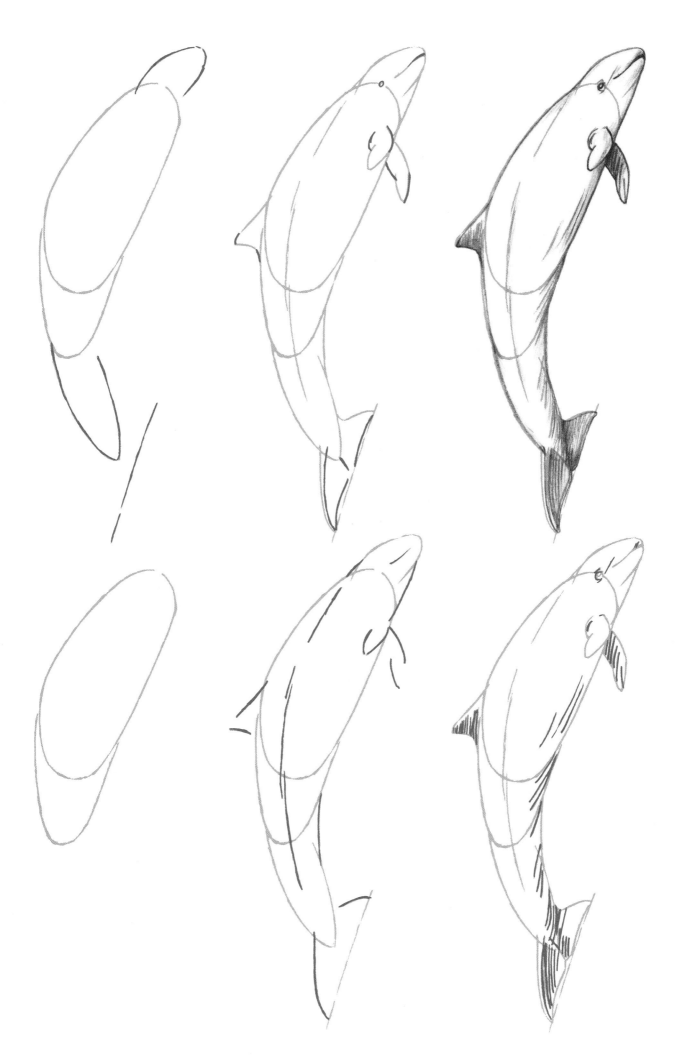

FALSE KILLER WHALE

Up to twenty feet long.
Belongs to dolphin family.

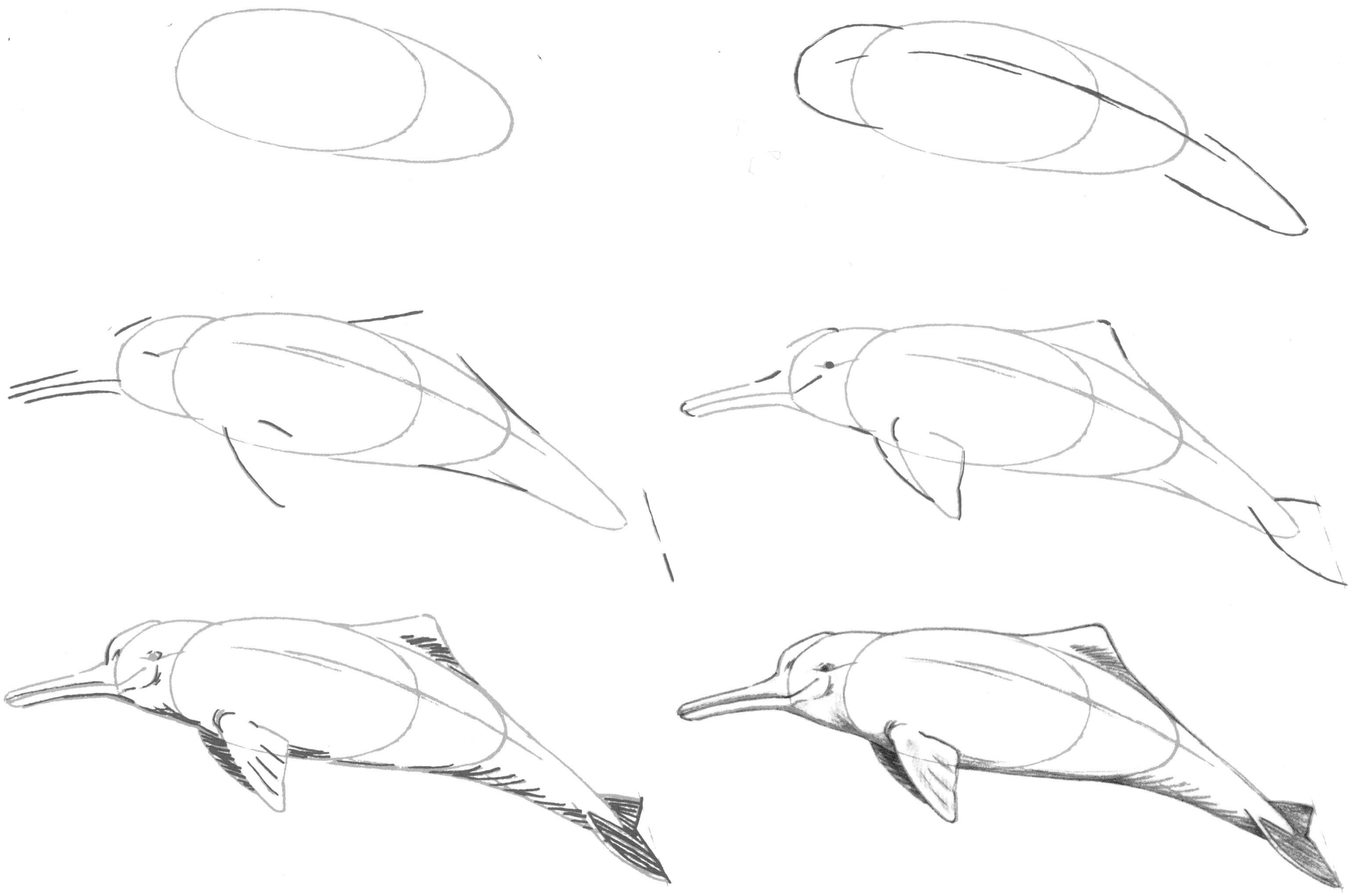

FRESHWATER DOLPHIN

Up to eight feet long

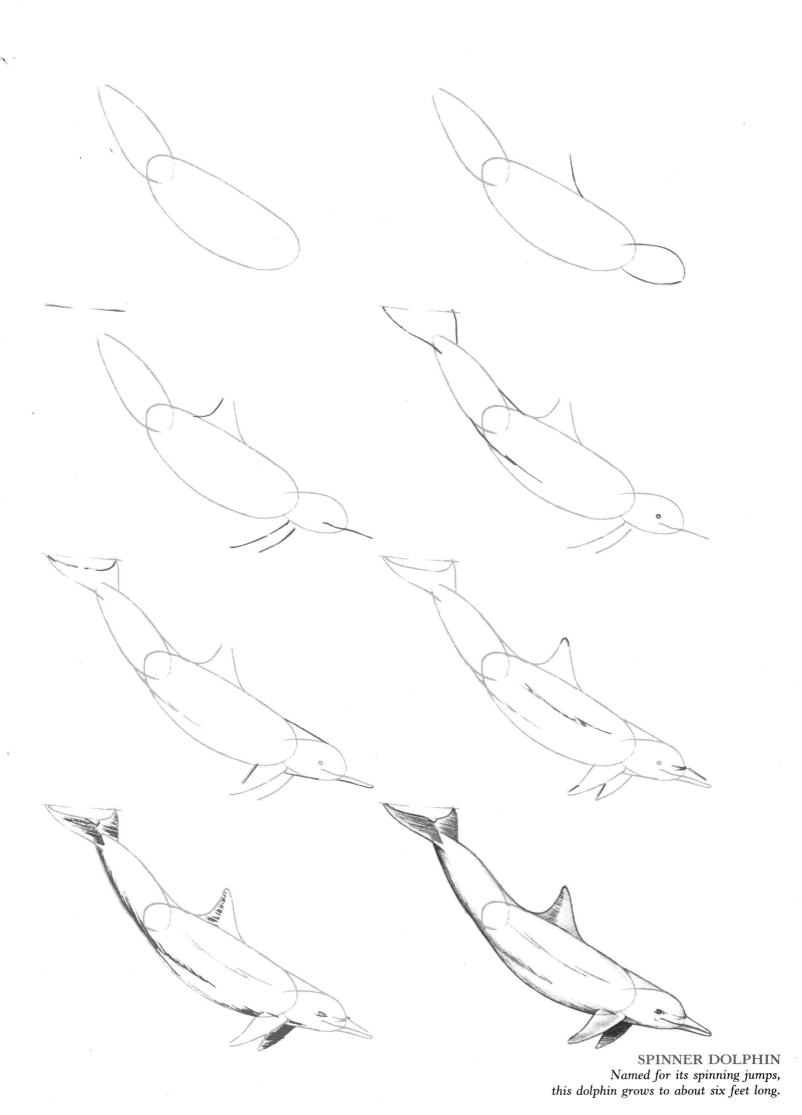

SPINNER DOLPHIN
Named for its spinning jumps,
this dolphin grows to about six feet long.

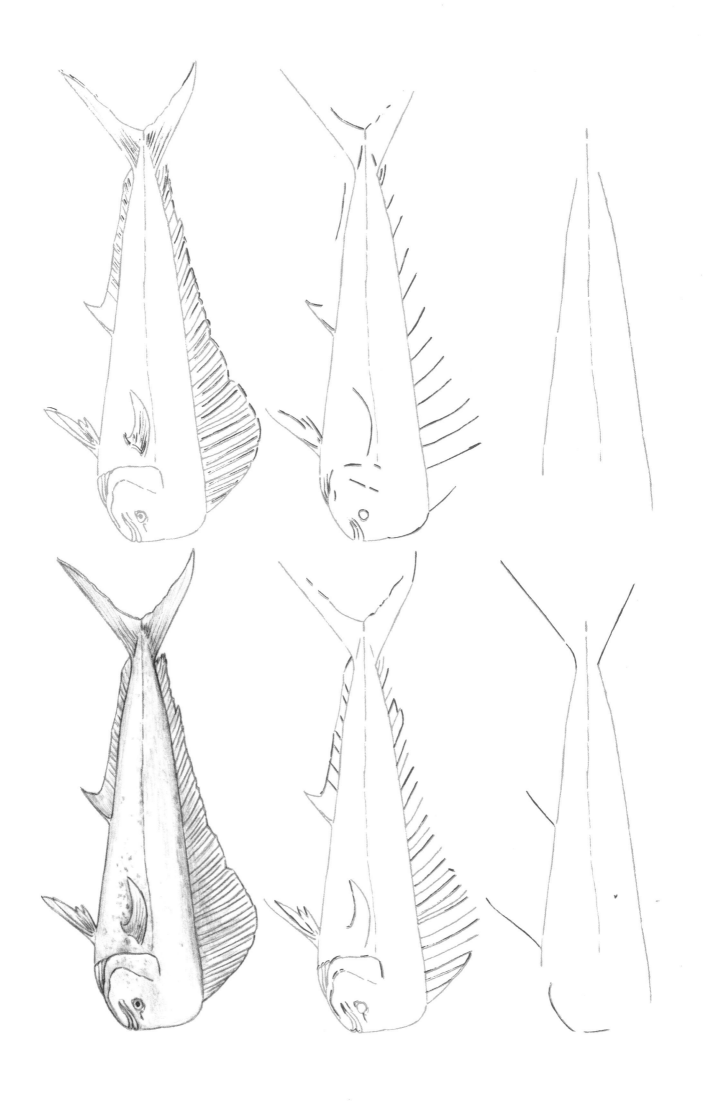

DOLPHIN FISH or **DORADO**
This dolphin is a fish, not a mammal.

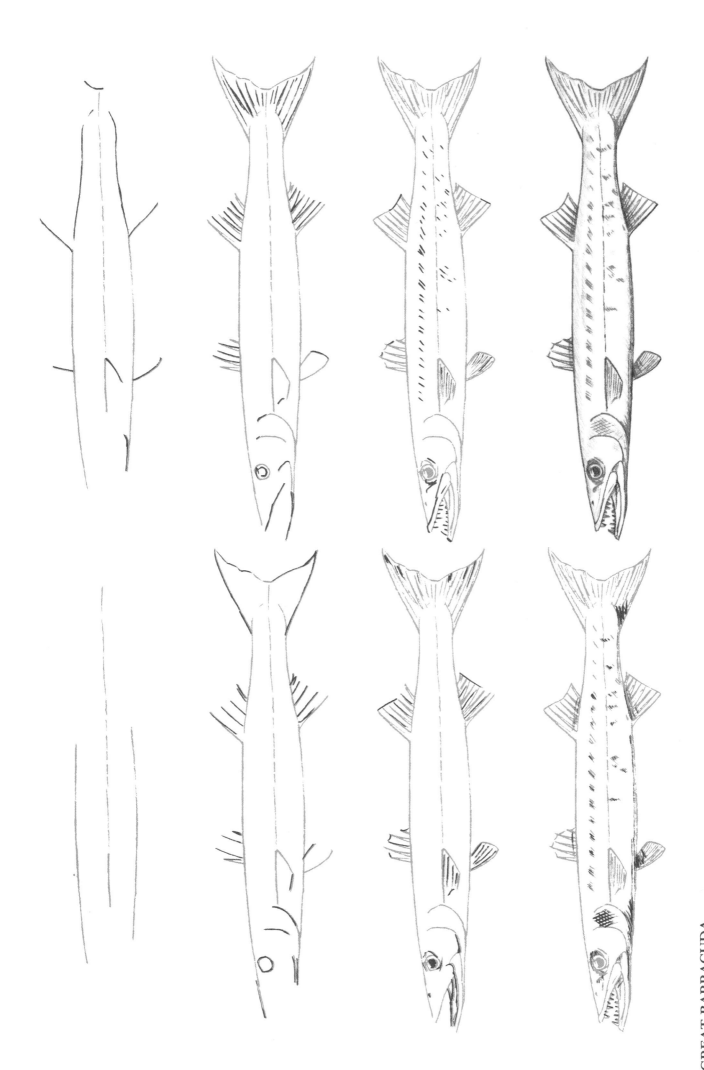

GREAT BARRACUDA
Up to ten feet long, this fish is capable of swimming
more than twenty-five miles per hour.

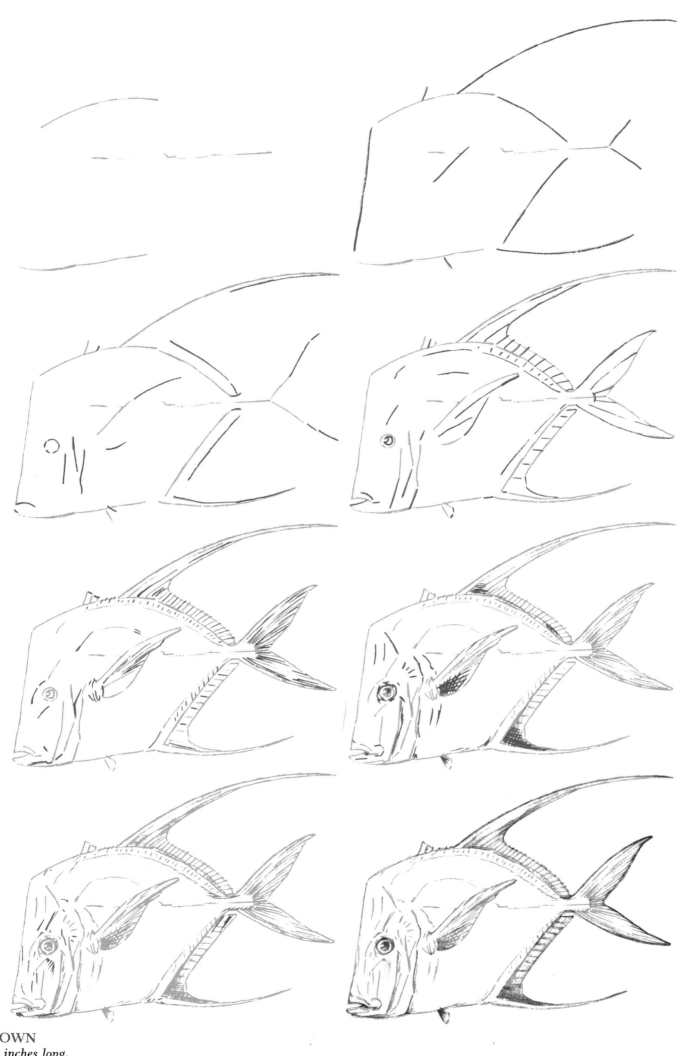

LOOK DOWN
Up to nine inches long,
the look down is a fierce fighting fish.

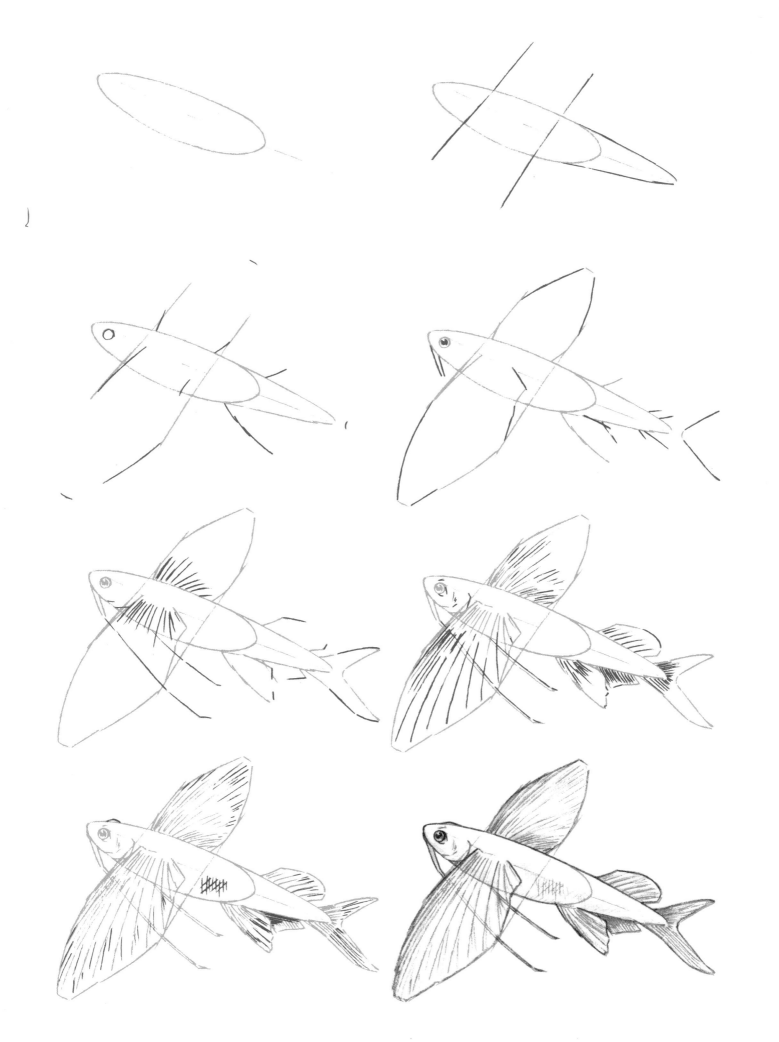

MARGINED FLYING FISH
Up to twelve inches long

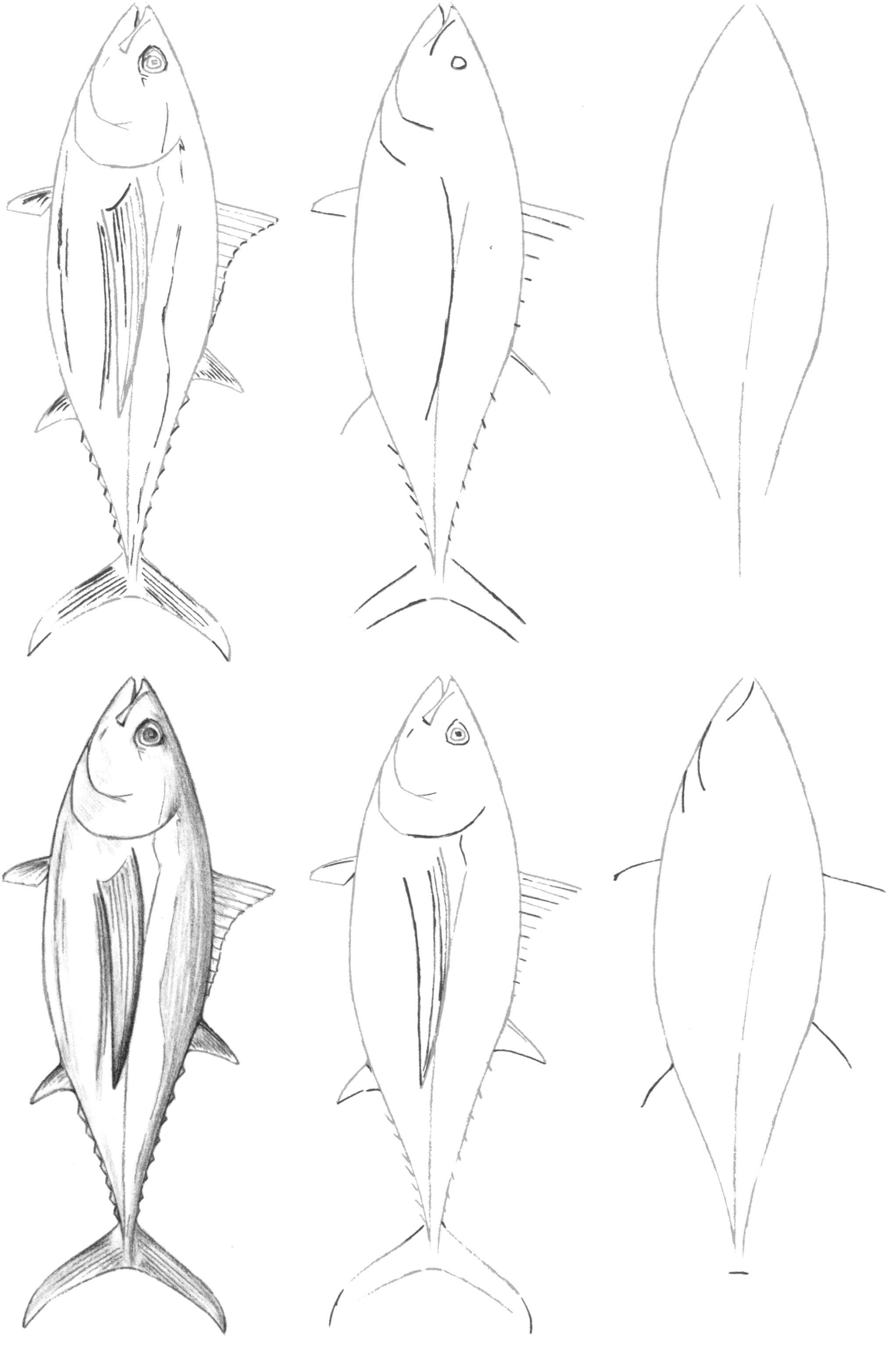

ALBACORE (LONGFIN) TUNA

Up to thirteen feet long

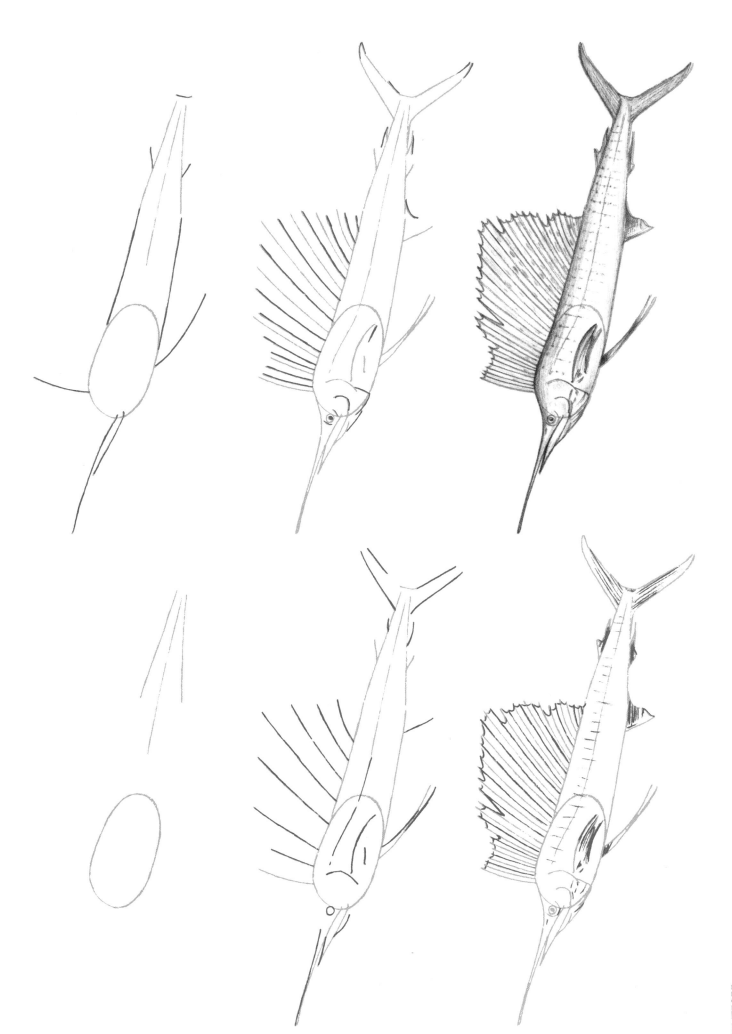

SAILFISH
Up to twelve feet long

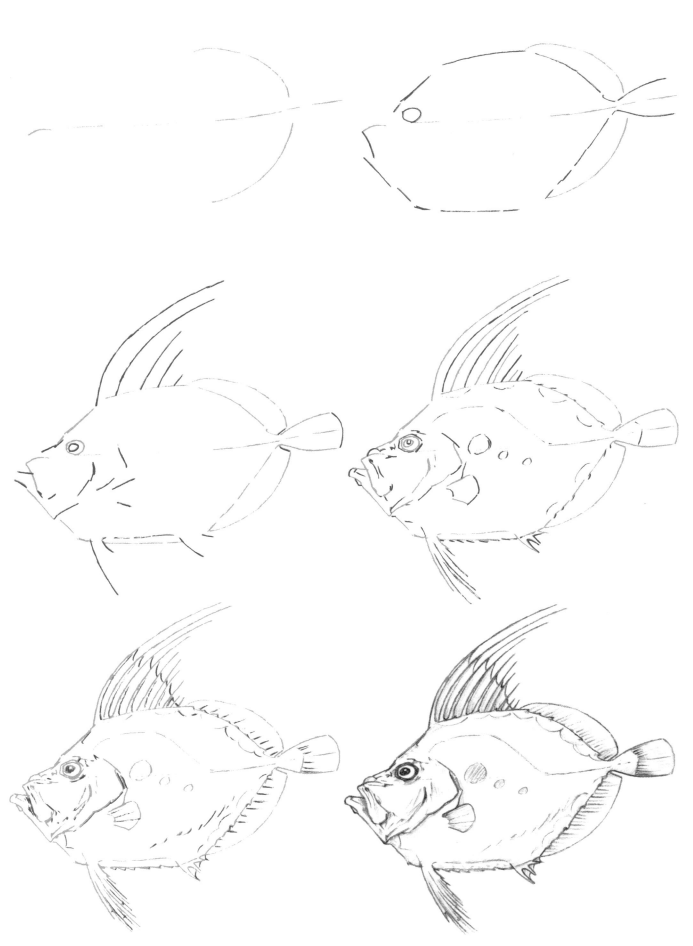

AMERICAN JOHN DORY
Up to twenty-four inches long,
this fish lives in water 1,200 feet deep.

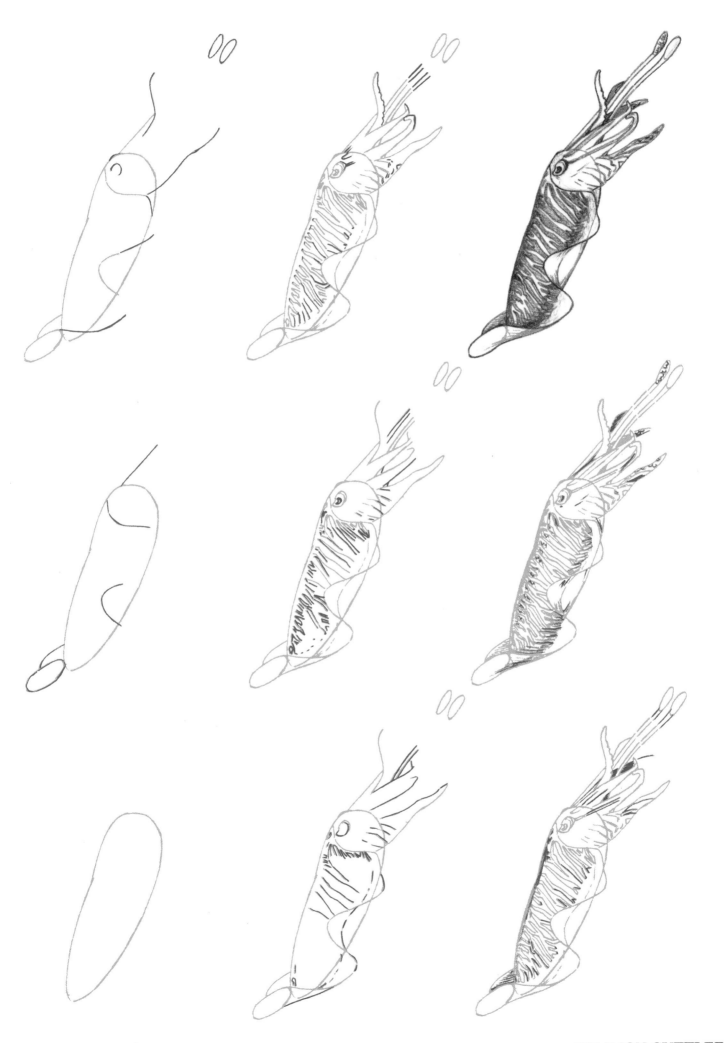

COMMON CUTTLEFISH
Up to twelve inches long

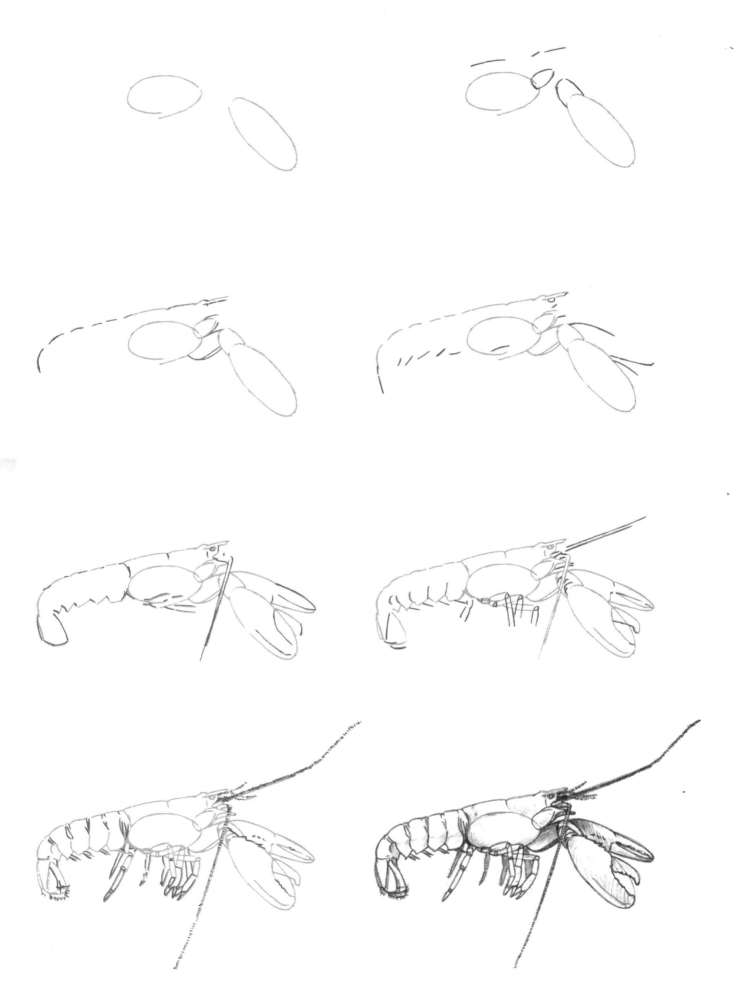

LOBSTER
*Classified as a **Crustacean**,*
lobsters can weigh up to five pounds.

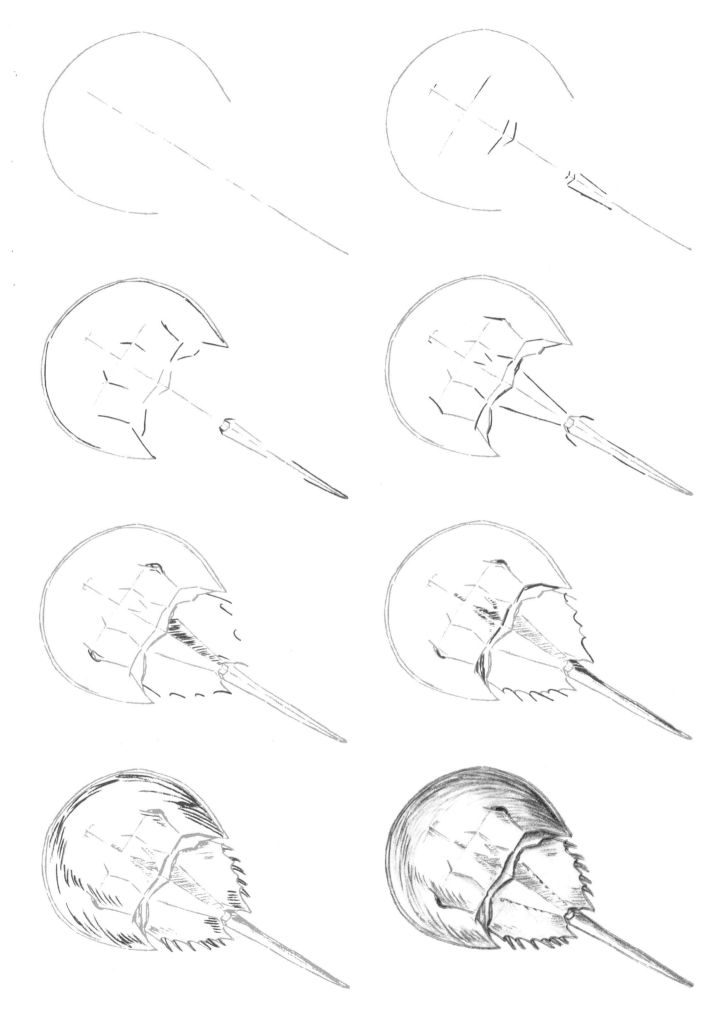

HORSESHOE CRAB
Up to three feet long

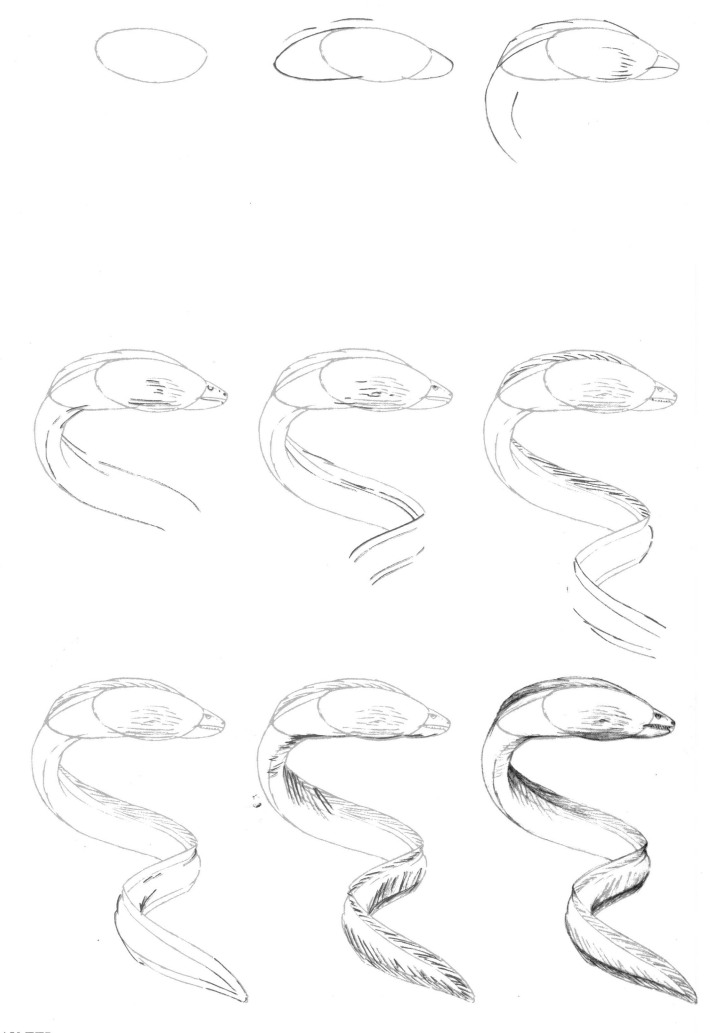

MORAY EEL
Up to six feet long

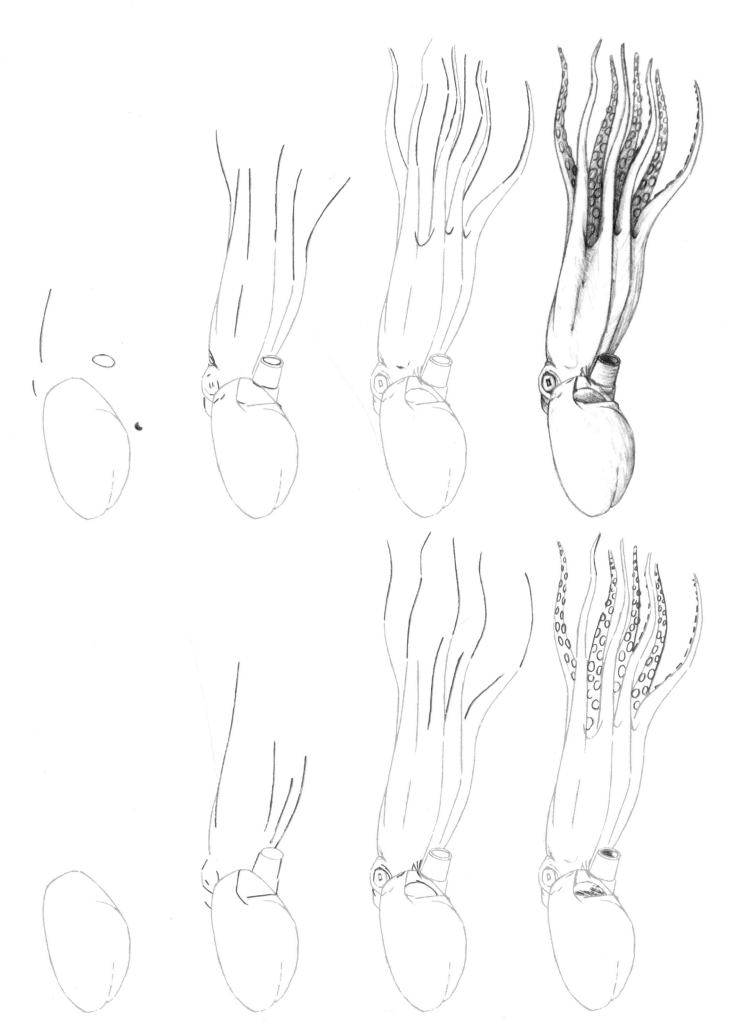

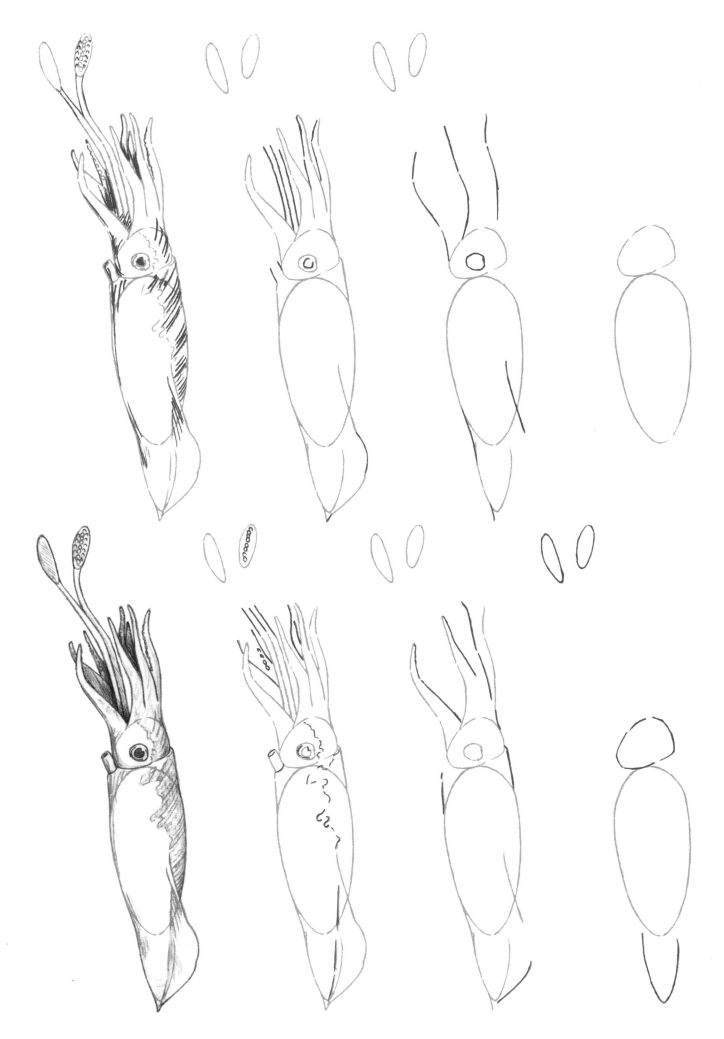

FRILLED SEA ANEMONE
Two to four inches tall

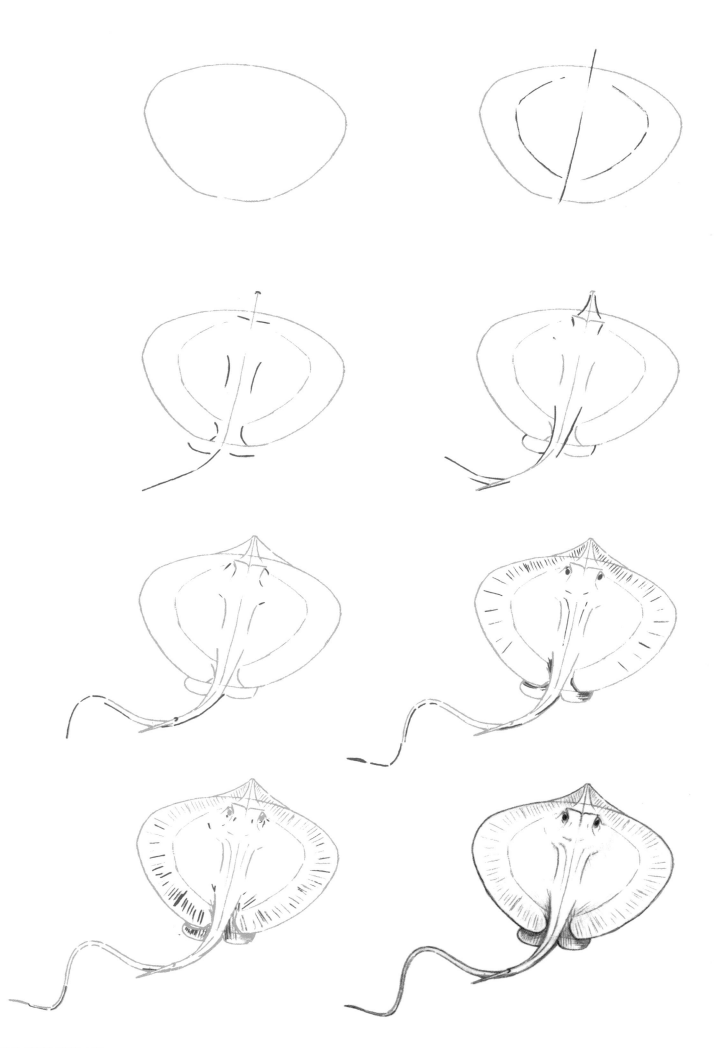

ATLANTIC STINGRAY
Up to seven feet long

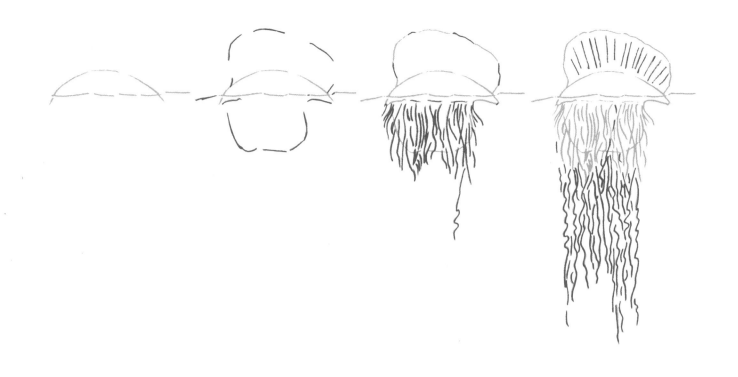

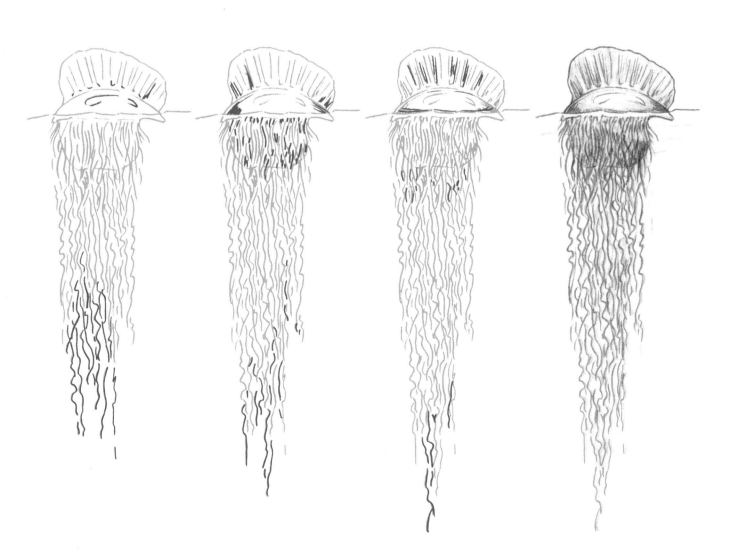

PORTUGUESE MAN-OF-WAR
Tentacles up to fifty feet long

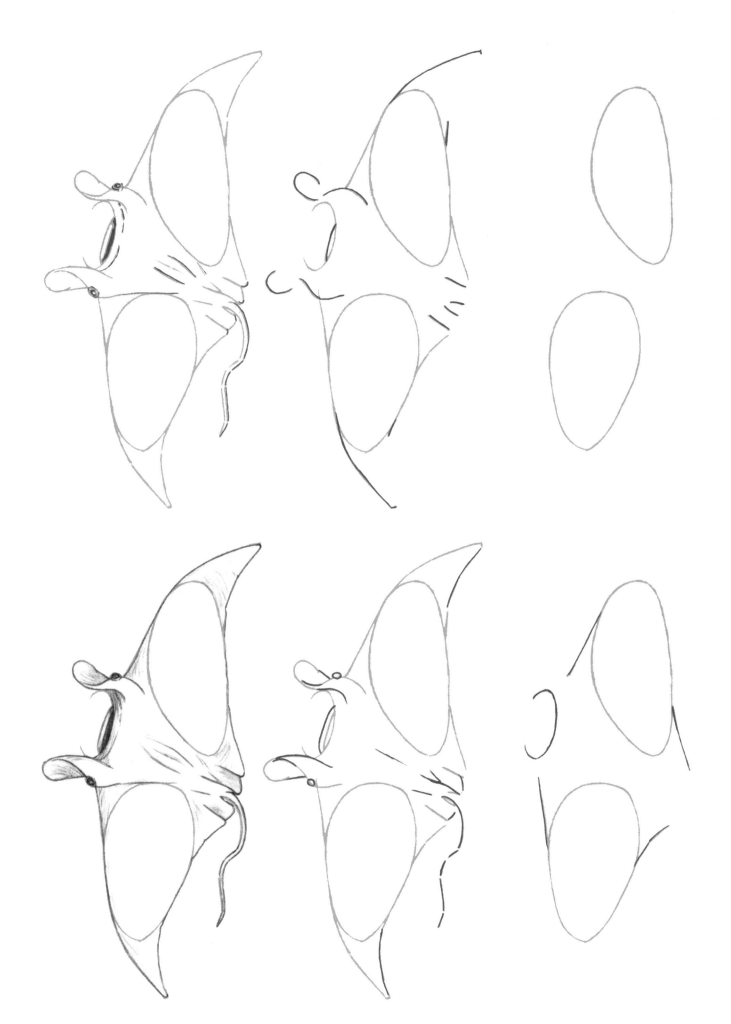

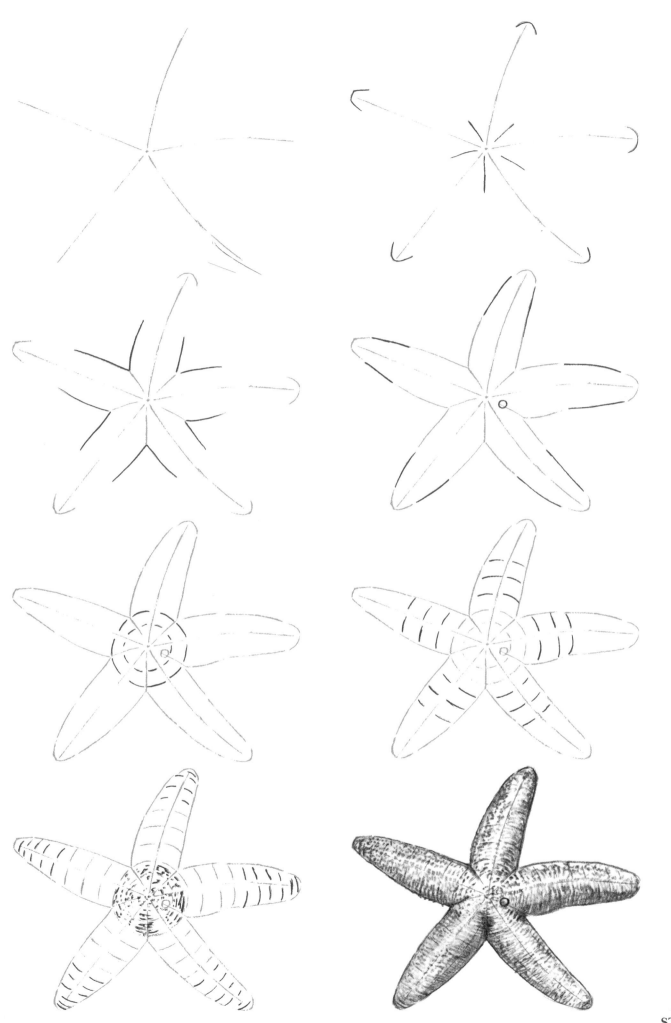

STARFISH

If the Starfish loses an arm, it grows back. Additionally, the arm that falls off will eventually become another Starfish.

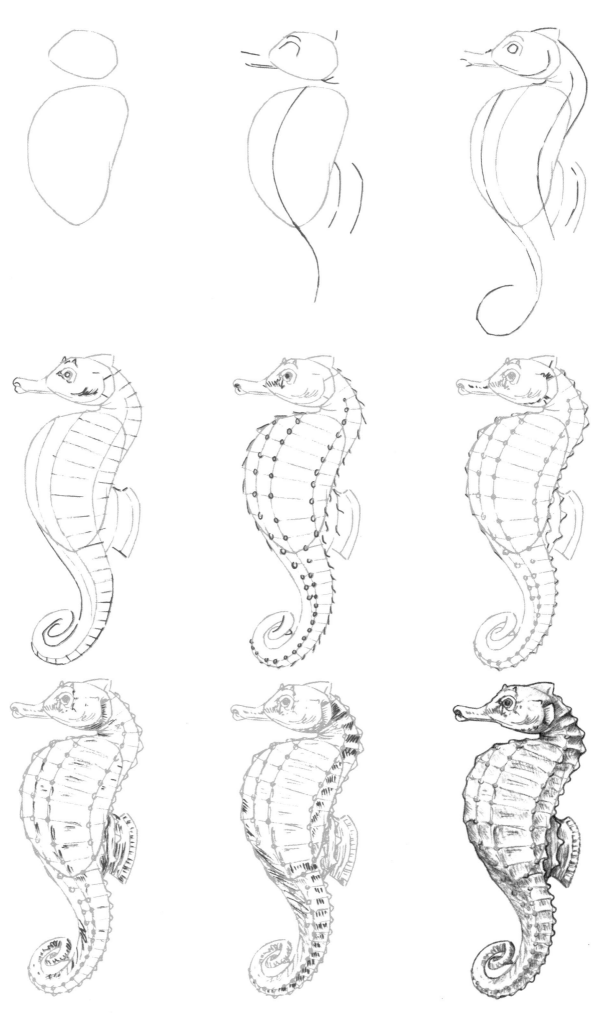

COMMON SEAHORSE (FEMALE)
*Unlike other sea creatures, the seahorse
swims upright. It grows up to eight inches long.*

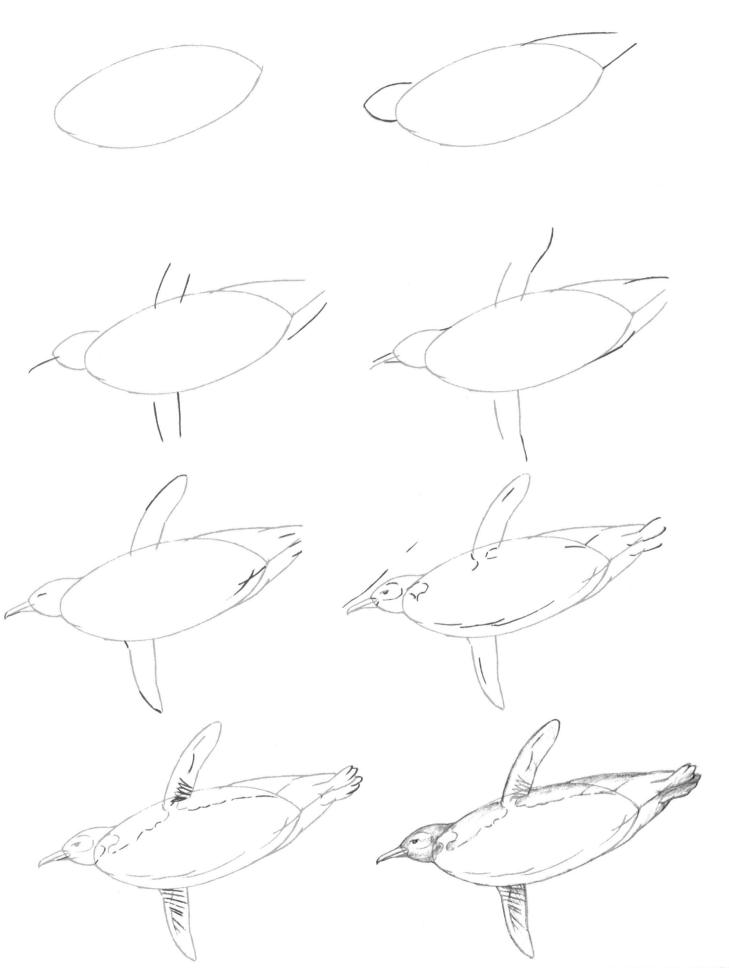

EMPEROR PENGUIN
*This oceangoing bird
grows up to four feet long.*

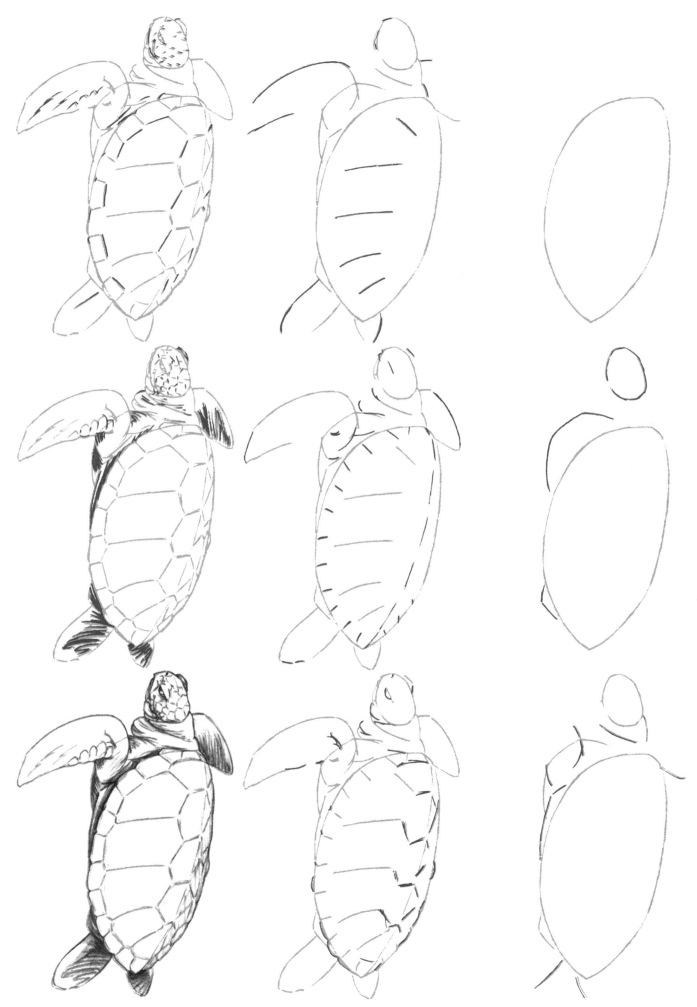

GREEN TURTLE
This sea turtle is a reptile
weighing up to five-hundred pounds.

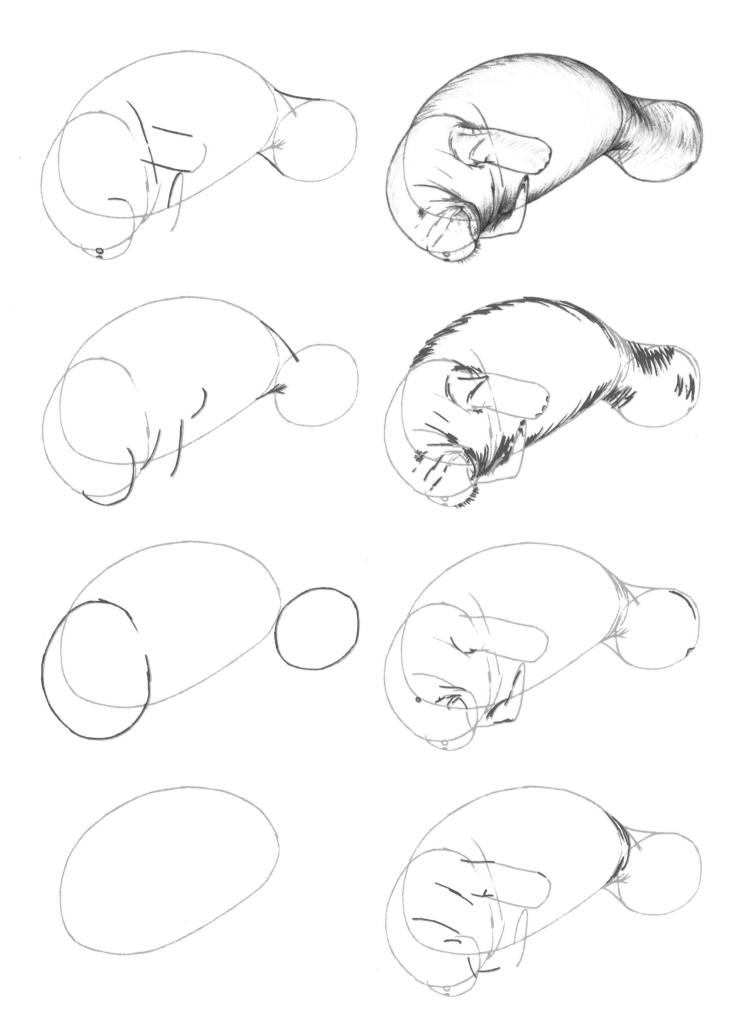

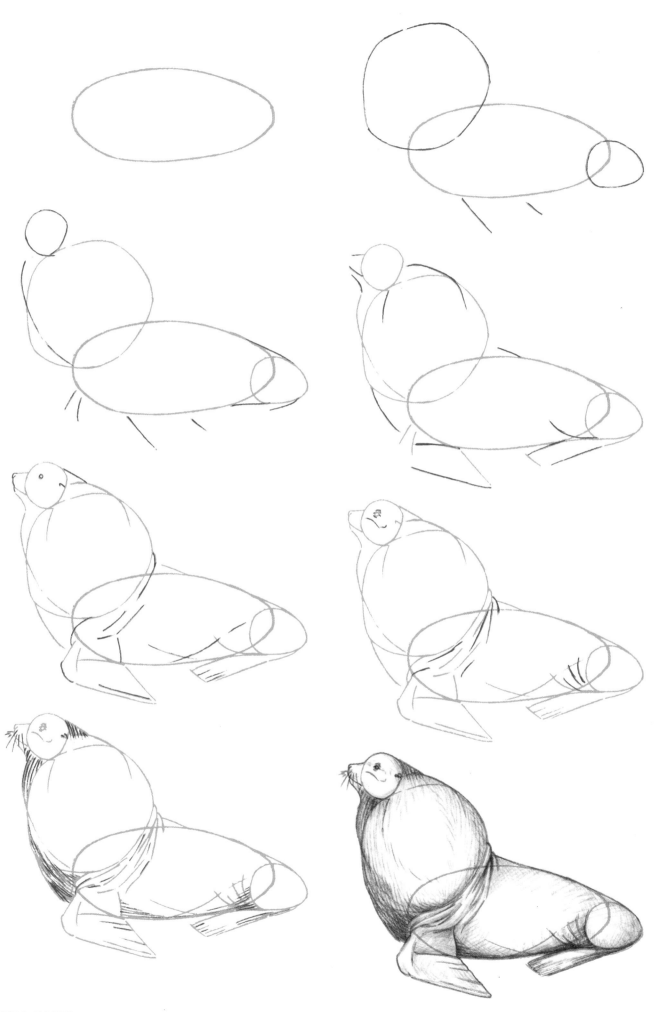

STELLAR SEA LION
This is the largest of the sea lions,
with the male weighing in at around one ton.

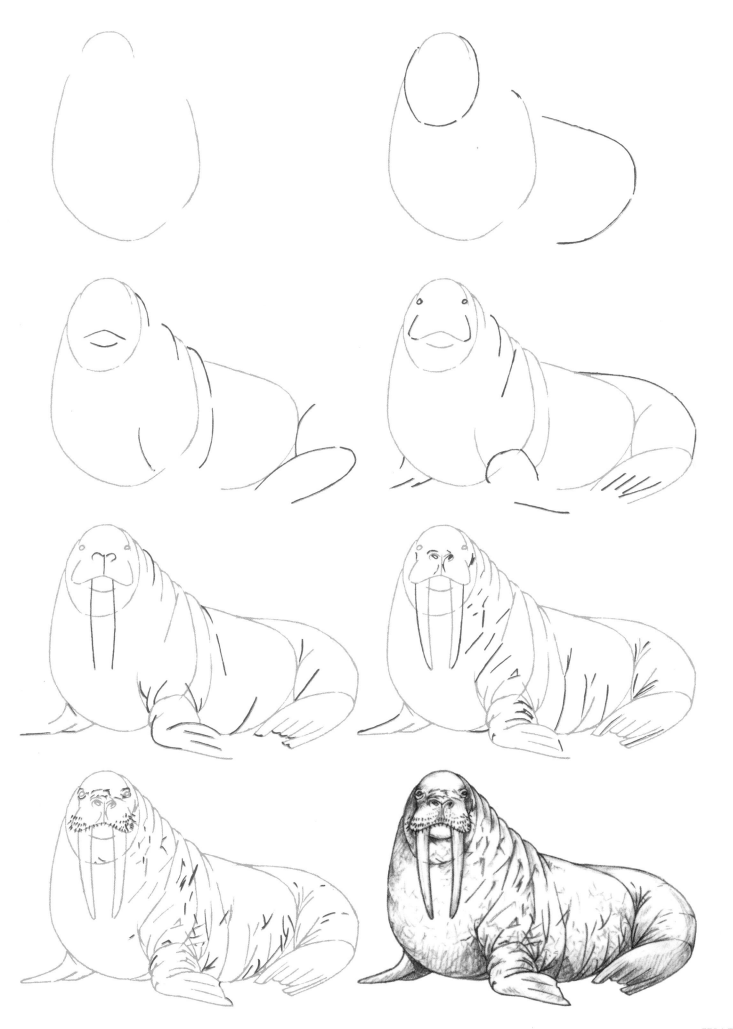

WALRUS
*All walruses have tusks and live
only in the Arctic (North Pole) waters.*

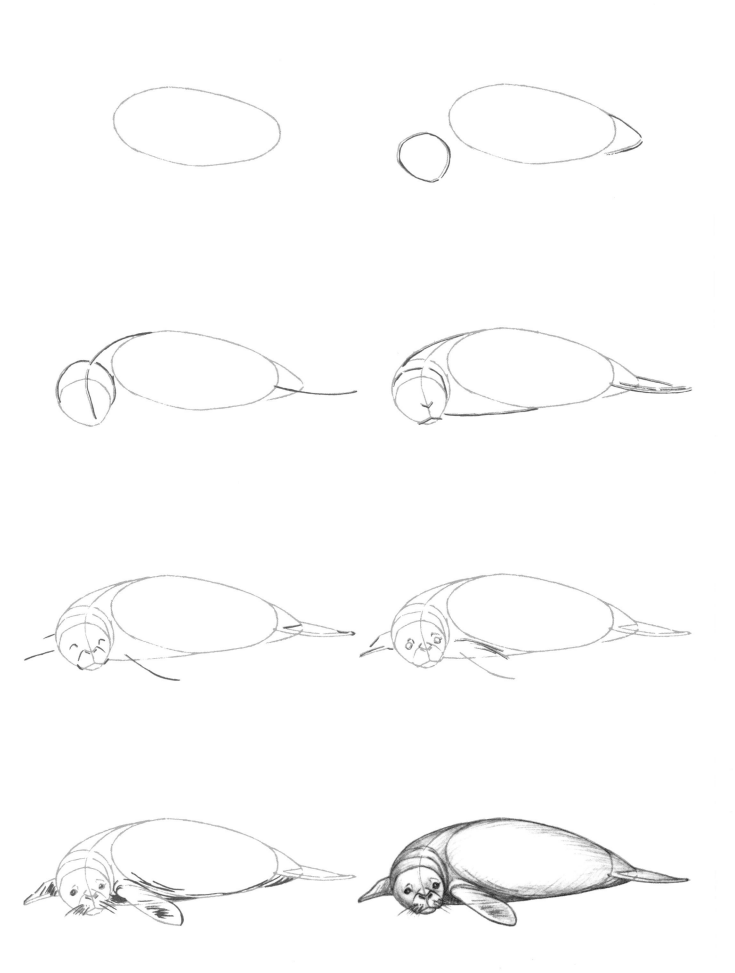

CARIBBEAN MONK SEAL
Unlike the sea lion, the seal has no ears.
It lives in water close to land.

LEE J. AMES joined the Doubleday list in 1962, and since that time his popular drawing books have sold nearly two million copies. Utilizing a unique step-by-step method to guide the young artist's hand, Ames's "Draw 50" books have inspired the creativity of countless children (and adults).

His artistic experience runs the gamut from working at Walt Disney Studios in the days when *Fantasia* and *Pinocchio* were created to teaching at New York City's School of Visual Arts to running his own advertising agency. In addition, he has illustrated over 150 books, from preschool picture books to postgraduate texts.

When not working in his studio, Lee can be found on the tennis courts of Long Island, New York, where he currently lives with his wife, Jocelyn.

Native Long Islander **WARREN BUDD** holds a bachelor's degree in fine arts from Southampton College. Primarily a natural science artist, he has been illustrating books for the past eight years. He and his wife, Christine, live on Long Island with their two children, Bryan and Drew.

DRAW 50 FOR HOURS OF FUN!

Using Lee J. Ames's proven, step-by-step method of drawing instruction, you can easily learn to draw animals, monsters, airplanes, cars, sharks, buildings, dinosaurs, famous cartoons, and so much more! Millions of people have learned to draw by using the award-winning "Draw 50" technique. Now you can too!

COLLECT THE ENTIRE DRAW 50 SERIES!

The Draw 50 Series books are available from your local bookstore. You may also order direct (make a copy of this form to order). Titles are paperback, unless otherwise indicated.

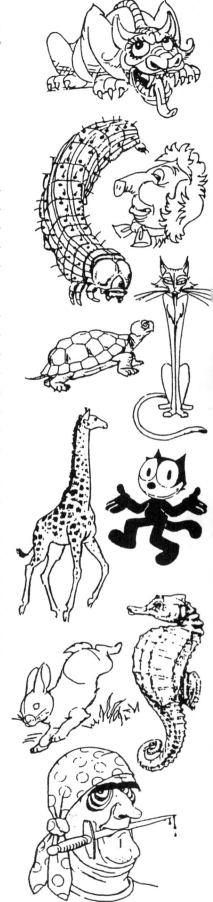

ISBN	TITLE	PRICE	QTY	TOTAL
23629-8	Airplanes, Aircraft, and Spacecraft	$8.95/$13.95 Can	× _____	= _____
49145-X	Aliens	$8.95/$13.95 Can	× _____	= _____
19519-2	Animals	$8.95/$13.95 Can	× _____	= _____
90544-X	Animal 'Toons	$8.95/$13.95 Can	× _____	= _____
24638-2	Athletes	$8.95/$13.95 Can	× _____	= _____
26767-3	Beasties and Yugglies and Turnover Uglies and Things That Go Bump in the Night	$8.95/$13.95 Can	× _____	= _____
47163-7	Birds	$8.95/$13.95 Can	× _____	= _____
47006-1	Birds (hardcover)	$13.95/$18.95 Can	× _____	= _____
23630-1	Boats, Ships, Trucks, and Trains	$8.95/$13.95 Can	× _____	= _____
41777-2	Buildings and Other Structures	$8.95/$13.95 Can	× _____	= _____
24639-0	Cars, Trucks, and Motorcycles	$8.95/$13.95 Can	× _____	= _____
24640-4	Cats	$8.95/$13.95 Can	× _____	= _____
42449-3	Creepy Crawlies	$8.95/$13.95 Can	× _____	= _____
19520-6	Dinosaurs and Other Prehistoric Animals	$8.95/$13.95 Can	× _____	= _____
23431-7	Dogs	$8.95/$13.95 Can	× _____	= _____
46985-3	Endangered Animals	$8.95/$13.95 Can	× _____	= _____
19521-4	Famous Cartoons	$8.95/$13.95 Can	× _____	= _____
23432-5	Famous Faces	$8.95/$13.95 Can	× _____	= _____
47150-5	Flowers, Trees, and Other Plants	$8.95/$13.95 Can	× _____	= _____
26770-3	Holiday Decorations	$8.95/$13.95 Can	× _____	= _____
17642-2	Horses	$8.95/$13.95 Can	× _____	= _____
17639-2	Monsters	$8.95/$13.95 Can	× _____	= _____
41194-4	People	$8.95/$13.95 Can	× _____	= _____
47162-9	People of the Bible	$8.95/$13.95 Can	× _____	= _____
47005-3	People of the Bible (hardcover)	$13.95/$19.95 Can	× _____	= _____
26768-1	Sharks, Whales, and Other Sea Creatures	$8.95/$13.95 Can	× _____	= _____
14154-8	Vehicles	$8.95/$13.95 Can	× _____	= _____
	Shipping and handling	**(add $2.50 per order)**	× _____	= _____
		TOTAL		_____

Please send me the title(s) I have indicated above. I am enclosing $_____.

Send check or money order in U.S. funds only (no C.O.D.s or cash, please). Make check payable to Random House, Inc. Allow 4–6 weeks for delivery. Prices and availability subject to change without notice.

Name: _____

Address: _____ Apt. #_____

City: _____ State: _____ Zip: _____

Send completed coupon and payment to:
Random House, Inc.
Customer Service
400 Hahn Rd.
Westminster, MD 21157

BROADWAY